Traditional English Session Tunes

with
Tablature for Anglo Concertina

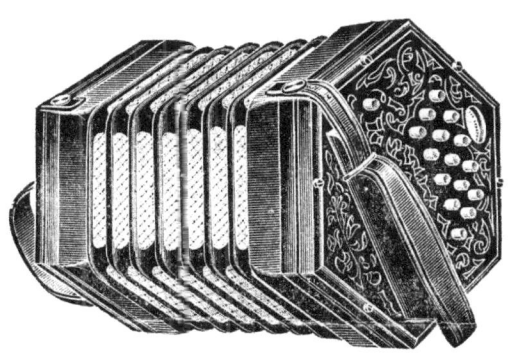

Gary Coover

ROLLSTON PRESS

Traditional English Session Tunes
by Gary Coover

All rights reserved. No part of this book may be reproduced, scanned, transmitted, or distributed in any printed or electronic form without the prior permission of the author except in the case of brief quotations embodied in articles or reviews.

Copyright © 2024 Gary Coover

ISBN-13: 978-1-953208-24-8

All titles are in the public domain unless otherwise noted.

Cover photo by the author: The White Hart
                             15th century coaching inn
                             St. Albans, England

ROLLSTON PRESS
1717 Ala Wai Blvd #1703
Honolulu, HI 96815
USA
www.rollstonpress.com

Table of Contents

INTRODUCTION 5
THE ENGLISH SESSION 6
KEYBOARD AND TABLATURE 7
CHORDS 8
TUNES
A Hundred Pipers... 10
Albert Farmer's Bonfire Tune 11
Astley's Ride... 12
Banbury Bill.. 13
Banks of the Dee.. 14
Beatrice Hill's Three-Handed Reel 15
Bonny Breast Knot..16
Bonny Kate.. 17
Brighton Camp..18
Buttered Peas 19
Captain Lanoe's Quick March 20
The Chestnut Tree 21
Clee Hill.. 22
Curly-Headed Ploughboy... 24
Donkey Riding.. 25
Dorset Four Hand Reel 26
Dorsetshire Hornpipe 28
Down the Road.. 30
Durham Rangers 32
Enrico 34
Fairy Dance 36
The Fiery Clockface 37
Galopede 38
Grandfather's Tune 40
Harper's Frolic 41
Horses Brawl 42
Hunting the Hare 44
Huntsman's Chorus... 46
Jamie Allen... 47

Jenny Lind	48
Keel Row	49
Lemmy Brazil's No. 2	50
Linnen Hall	52
Little Diamond	53
Man in the Moon	54
Michael Turner's Waltz	55
New Rigged Ship	56
Off She Goes	57
Orange in Bloom	58
The Oyster Girl	60
Portsmouth	61
Princess Royal	62
The Quaker	63
Rakes of Mallow	64
The Railway	65
Redowa Polka	66
Rochdale Coconut Dance	68
Rogue's March	69
The Roman Wall	70
The Rose Tree	71
Roxborough Castle	72
Salmon Tails up the Water	74
Scan Tester's Polka No. 2	75
Seven Stars	76
Shepton Mallett Hornpipe	77
The Sloe	78
Smash the Windows	79
Speed the Plough	80
Three Around Three	82
Tip Top Polka	83
Uncle Bernard's	84
Walter Bulwer's Polka No. 1	85
Walter Bulwer's Polka No. 2	86
Winster Gallop	87
Woodland Revels	88
Young May Moon	91

Introduction

Traditional English tunes have been played in many different keys over the years, but session tunes today tend to be mostly in the keys of G and D since these keys are preferred by fiddlers and are the home keys of the popular 2-row D/G button accordion known as a melodeon.

This can be frustrating for players of the C/G Anglo concertina, and although many folks also own G/D concertinas, they are fairly rare when compared to the number of C/G instruments available.

So, if you have a C/G Anglo and want to play in English sessions, then this book is designed especially for you!

All 65 tunes here are in the keys of G and D, and in the keys they are typically played in at most sessions. Two-thirds of the tunes are in the key of G, and nearly half can be played on a 20-button C/G Anglo.

For many of the tunes in G, you might be able to play the whole tune on just the bottom G-row of the concertina, give it a try!

Notation and tablature will help you play the melodies – other instruments in sessions typically provide the backup chordal accompaniment. However, chord symbols are also provided if you'd like to add, punch in, or just chord along.

A few of the button number choices might seem unusual – in some cases they were chosen to make it easier to add left hand chords if you want.

Button numbers are suggestions only, not absolutes, and the tablature is just a crutch to help you get started. The tablature here shows only one way of playing the tune, not the only way. Feel free to find alternate buttons in other places and adapt to your playing style.

Dots and tablature are great for beginners, but the goal is to play music and not just push buttons. Listen to how others are playing, learn as much as you can by ear, and use the bellows to breathe life into the tunes.

If you eventually learn to read music notation on the Anglo it will open up a whole new world for you – hundreds of books with thousands of pages of wonderful tunes to choose from.

All of the tunes in this book have QR code links to a wide variety of traditional musicians playing the tune – from solo fiddlers to full sessions to loud folkrock – with many featuring the free-reed cousin of the concertina, the D/G melodeon. A couple of the videos even have steam-powered percussion!

English traditional music is great fun to play, and sessions can be delightful social events. I hope this book helps you get started on learning how to join in and play along with your C/G Anglo concertina.

The English Session

English sessions are very different from typical Irish sessions. Although both feature traditional music played on traditional instruments (mostly), English sessions tend to be more relaxed and more fun for both players and listeners.

The traditional English music session is most often a weekly or monthly occurrence found in pubs, and it is an informal gathering of musicians of all skill levels who enjoy playing traditional music together as a group.

The pace of the tunes tends to be slower than those found in Irish sessions, with far more hornpipes, stepdances, jigs, schottisches and marches than fast reels.

In Irish sessions, each tune is typically played exactly three times through before changing to several others, with many medleys having predetermined sets.

Instead of rushing through lots of tunes, English sessions typically concentrate on one tune at a time, sometimes at great length. Some tunes are often paired together, but medleys are rare. Most players prefer to explore the possibilities of one tune through many repetitions, giving everyone a chance to participate.

"If a tune's worth playing once it's worth playing a hundred times"

John Kirkpatrick

The theory being, play the tune until you are totally bored with it – and then keep playing. Only then will you discover all that it has to offer.

English sessions are very inclusive, and are not limited to just fiddles, guitars, mandolins, harmonicas, whistles, concertinas, and melodeons – you might also see saxophones, hammered dulcimers, and even high-hat cymbals and tubas!

Be aware that traditional tunes can be known by many different names, and tunes often have local and regional variations, so adapt when necessary. Also, rhythm and phrasing are far more important than speed.

Learning from "the dots" is no substitute for learning with your ears, since sheet music cannot teach style and only presents one version. The whole point of extended playing of one tune is to appreciate and explore.

Session styles can vary from place to place, and all seem to have different unwritten guidelines, so it's better to observe first before barging in.

Always strive to blend in rather than dominate – you want to be invited back again, right? Shine when appropriate, but blending in is the key to good music and good relations at a typical music session.

And most important of all, enjoy the tunes and the people you are playing with!

Keyboard & Tablature

The button numbering system for the 30-button Anglo concertina in C/G:

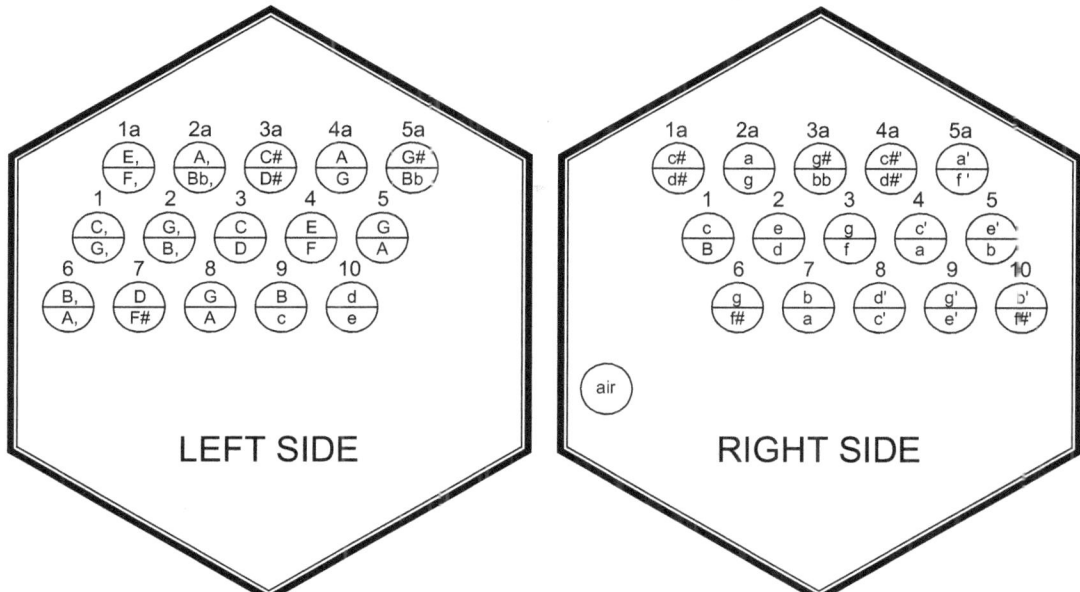

Low notes are on the left side of the instrument and high notes are on the right. Notes shown above the line are on the push, notes shown below the line are on the pull. Standard abc notation has been used to show the pitches of the notes.

How the tablature works:

- The buttons are numbered "1a-10" for each side.
- Buttons on the right-hand side are shown above the musical notes.
- Buttons on the left-hand side are shown below the musical notes.
- Notes on the push are shown by button number only.
- Notes on the pull are shown by button number with a line across the top.
- Long phrases all on the pull will have one long continuous line above the button numbers.

EXAMPLE:

Each tune also has a Button Map showing the buttons needed to play that particular tune:

Buttons played

Traditional English Session Tunes

Chords

There will probably be times when you might want to simply "chord along" instead of playing the tune – perhaps you want to incorporate some chordal accompaniment with the melody, or maybe because you don't know the tune but still want to join in.

You don't always have all the notes of the chords, and in the same direction, on the Anglo concertina, but you do have lots of choices where chords or partial chords exist in both directions. You don't need to play every note of the chord. Fewer notes, or the "open fifth" chord often work much better.

Here are the most common chords in the keys of G and D, and where to find them on a C/G Anglo concertina:

Left Hand Chords

KEY	I	IV	V	V7	vi	open 5th
G	G 1-2-3-4a	C 1-3-4-5	D 3-7-5/8	D7 3-7-5/8-9	Em 1a-4-5-9	G modal 1-3-4a
	G 2-8-9-10	C 4a-9-10	D* 7-4a-10 * partial chord			G modal 2-8-10
D	D 3-7-5/8	G 1-2-3-4a	A 2a-3a-4-4a	A7 2a-3a-4-5	Bm 2-3-7	D modal 3-5
	D* 7-4a-10 * partial chord	G 2-8-9-10				D modal 7-2a

Traditional English Session Tunes

TUNES

A Hundred Pipers

Buttons played

Traditional

Albert Farmer's Bonfire Tune

Buttons played

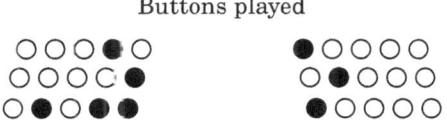

Traditional

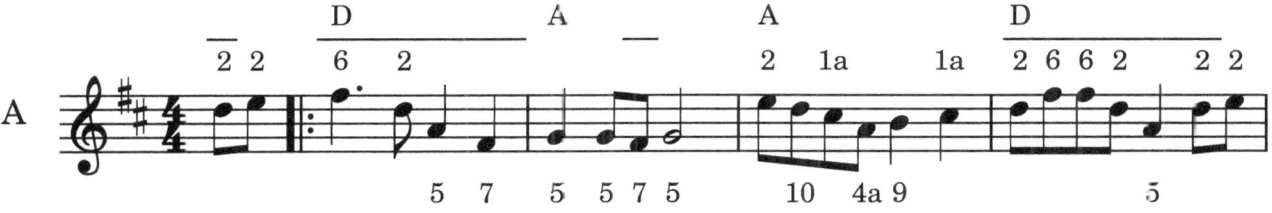
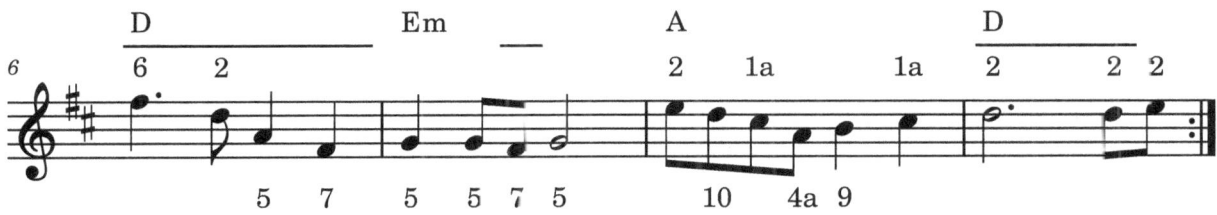

Astley's Ride

Traditional

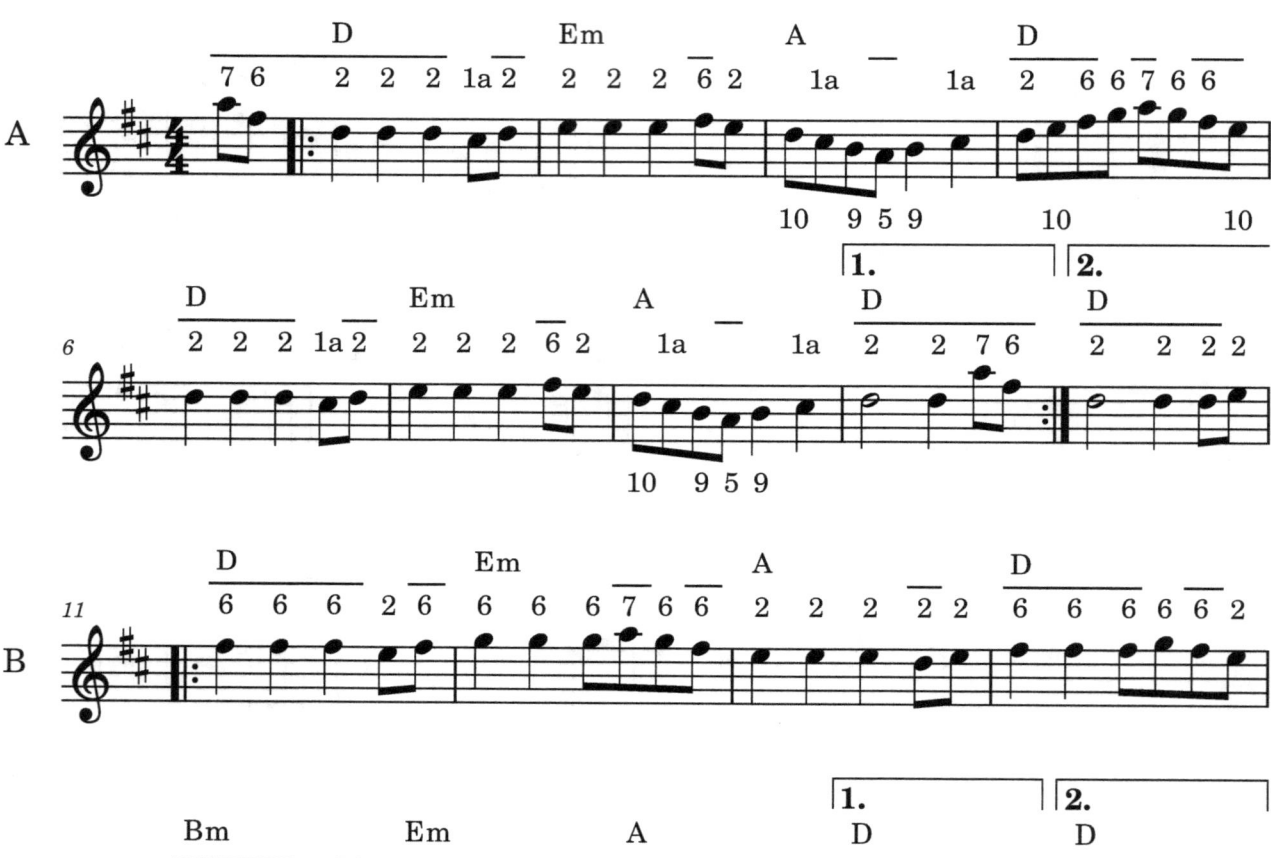

Banbury Bill

Buttons played

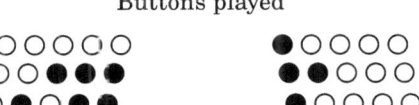

Traditional

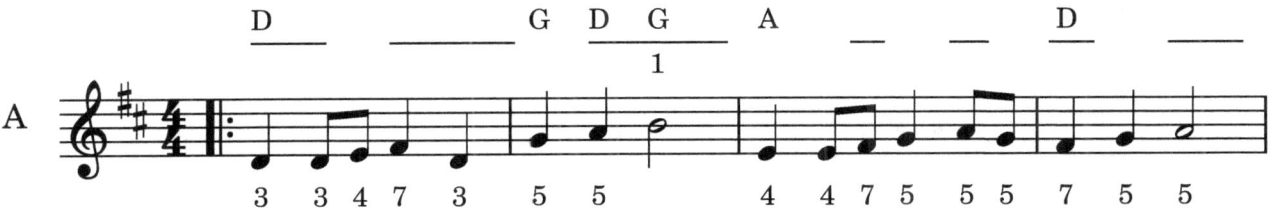

Banks of the Dee

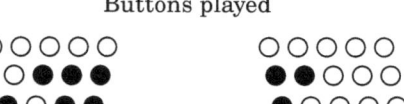

Buttons played

Traditional

Beatrice Hill's Three-Handed Reel

Bonny Breast Knot

Buttons played

Traditional

Bonny Kate

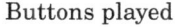

Traditional

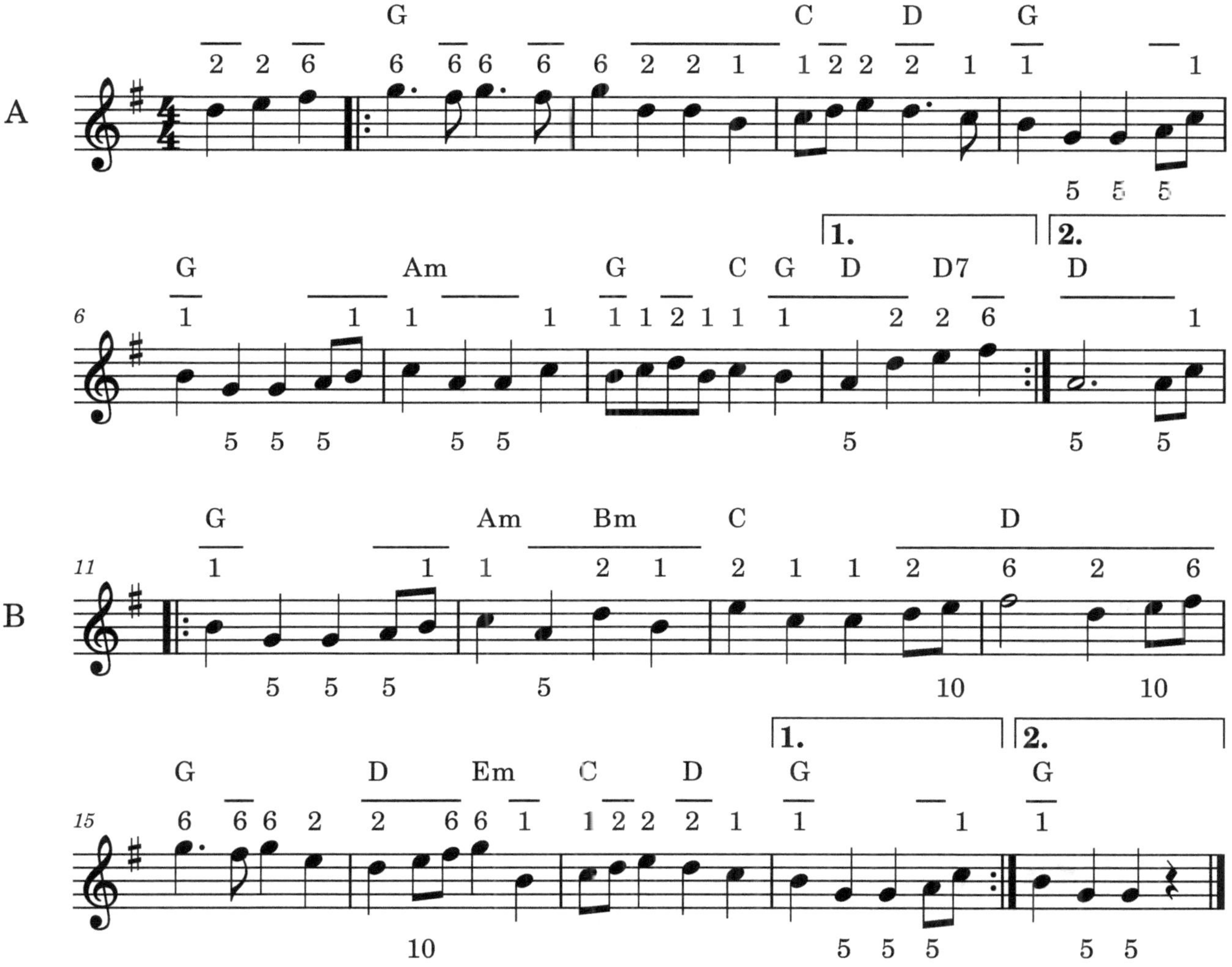

Brighton Camp

Buttons played
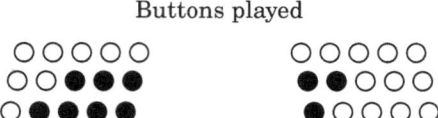

Traditional

Buttered Peas

Buttons played

Traditional

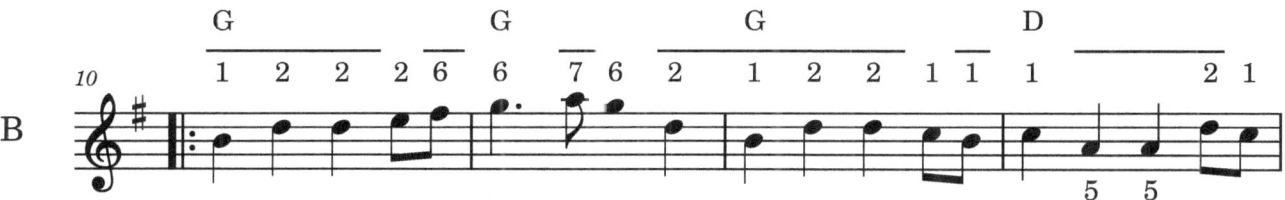

Captain Lanoe's Quick March

The Chestnut Tree

Clee Hill

Buttons played

Traditional

Traditional English Session Tunes

The Curly-Headed Ploughboy

Buttons played

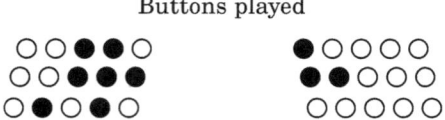

Traditional

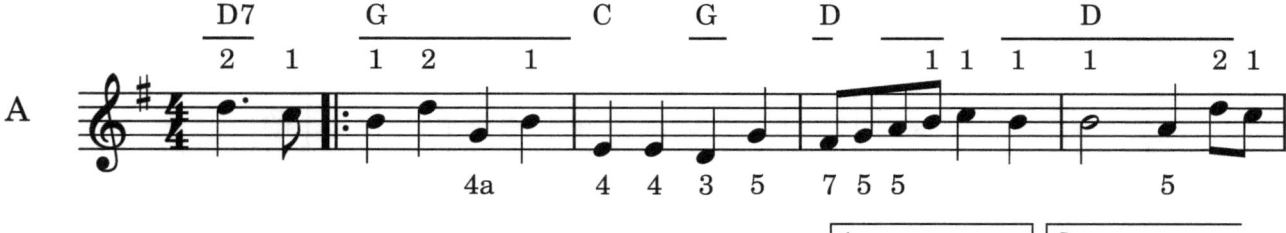
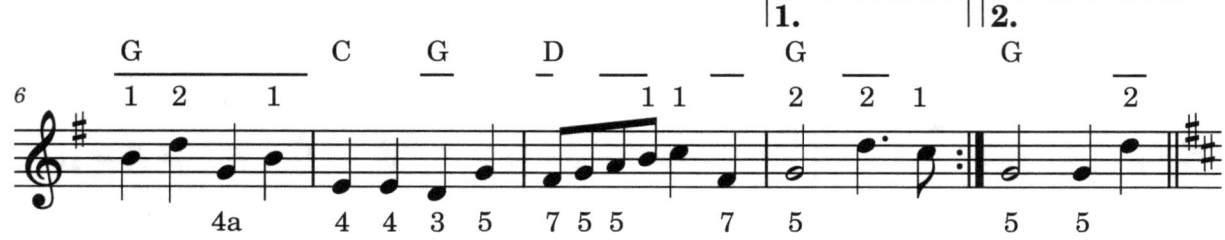
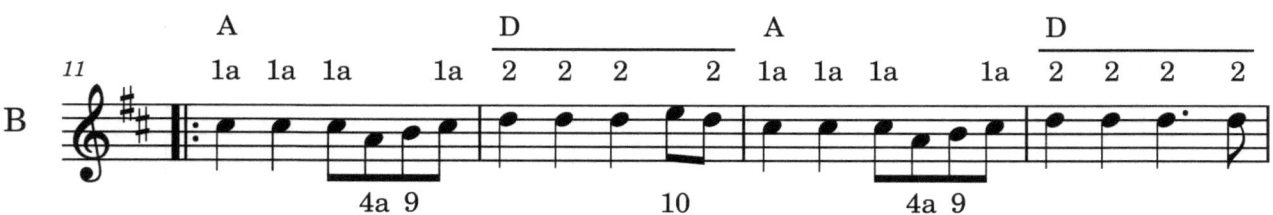

Traditional English Session Tunes

Donkey Riding

Buttons played

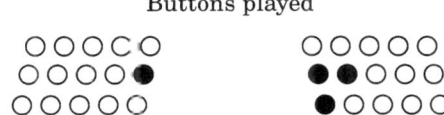

Traditional

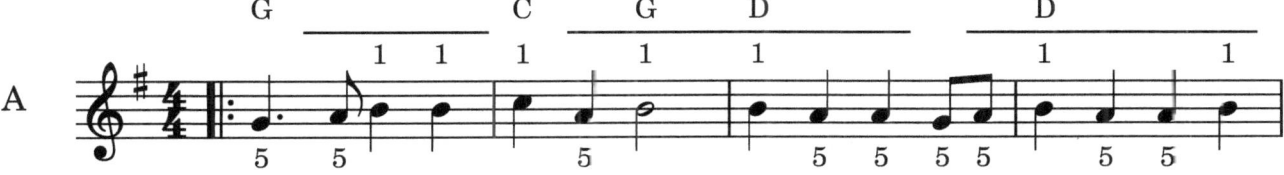

Dorset Four Hand Reel

Buttons played

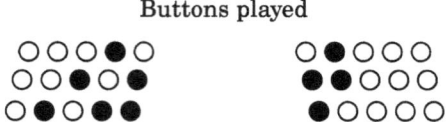

Traditional

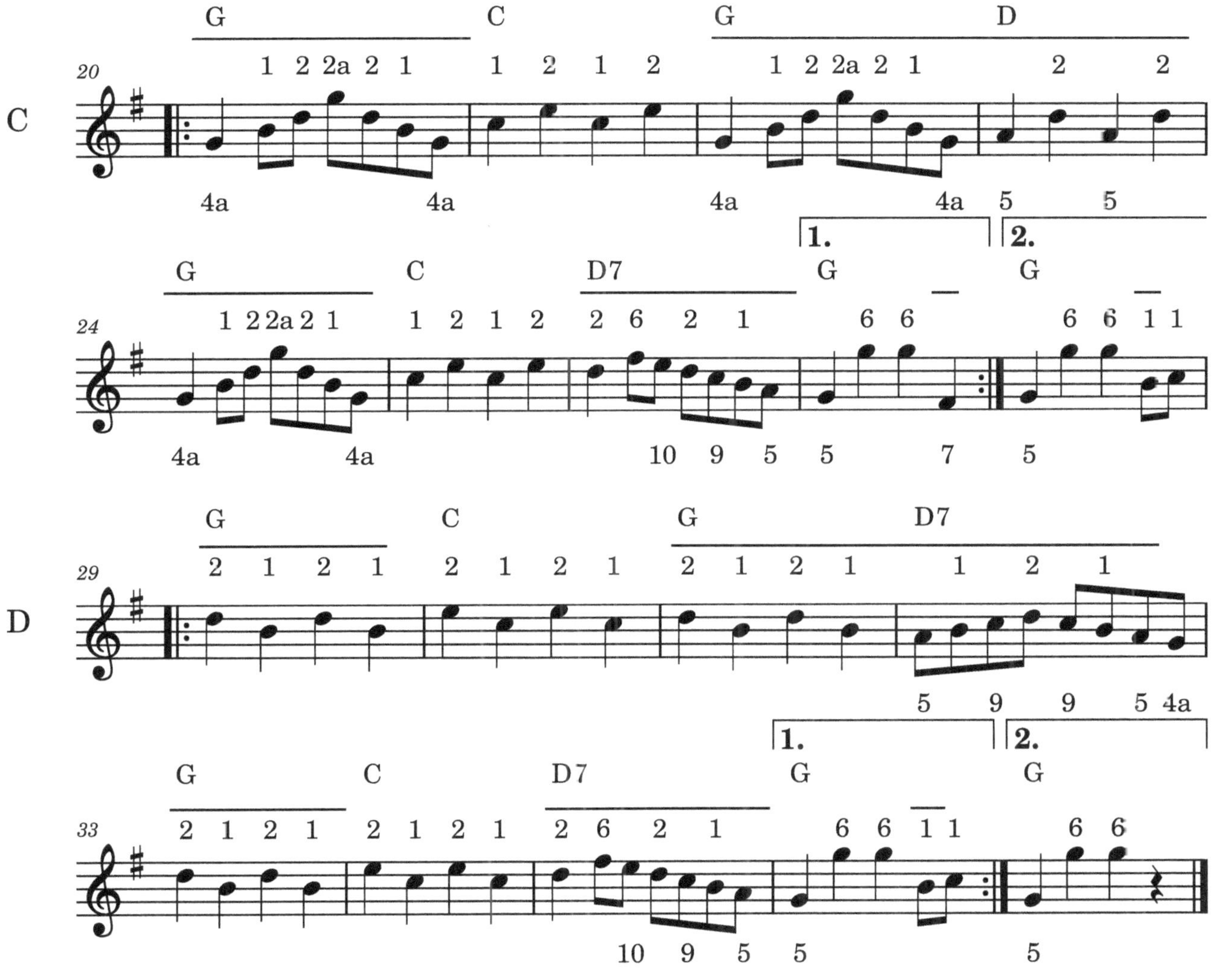

The Dorsetshire Hornpipe

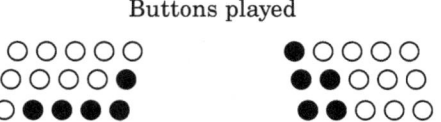

Traditional

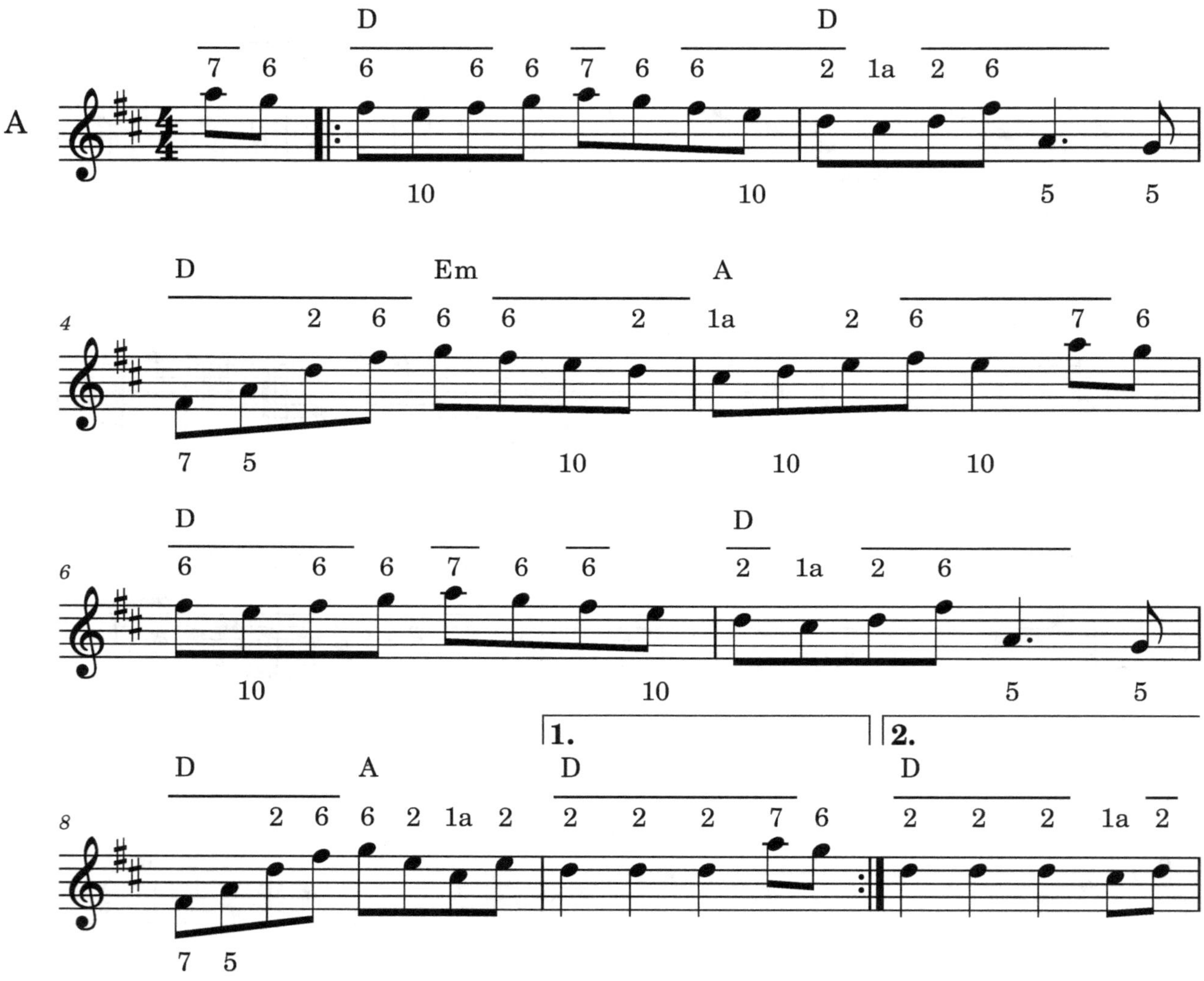

Traditional English Session Tunes

Down the Road

Buttons played

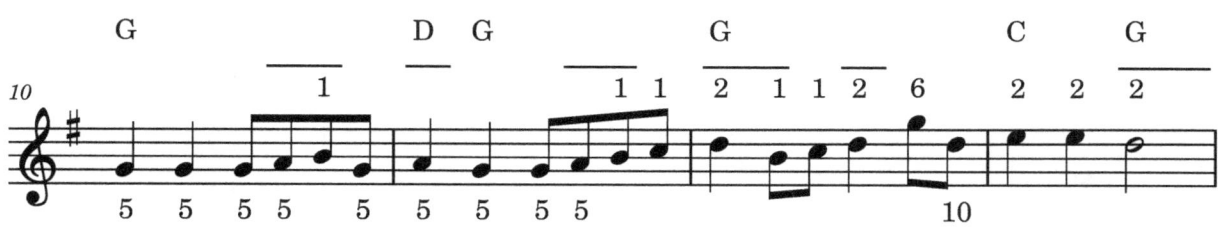

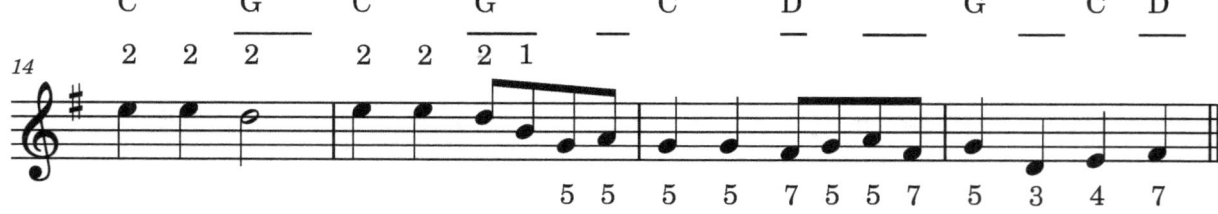

Traditional English Session Tunes

Durham Rangers

Buttons played

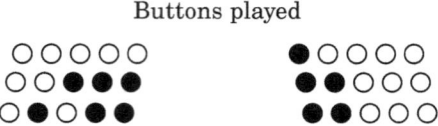

Traditional

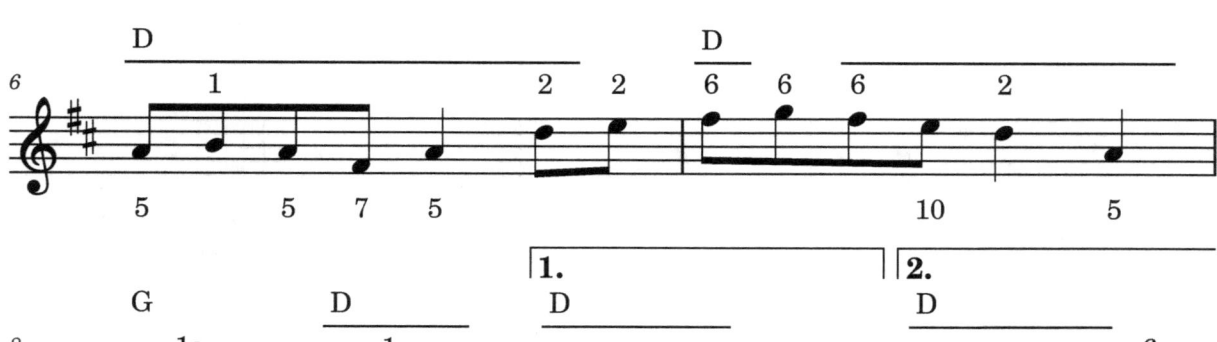
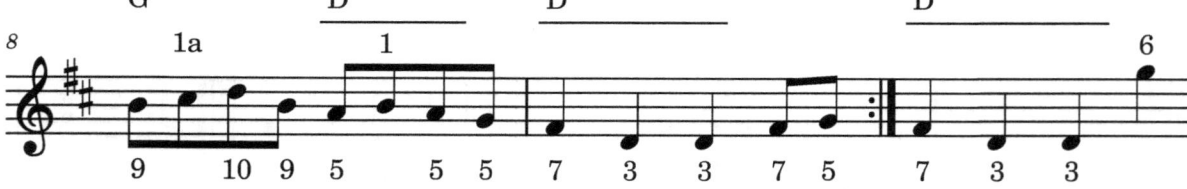

Traditional English Session Tunes

Enrico

Buttons played
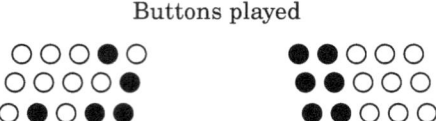

Traditional

Fairy Dance

The Fiery Clock Face

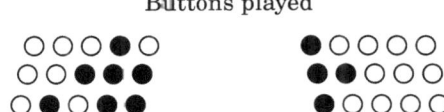

Buttons played

Traditional

Galopede

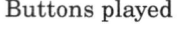

Traditional

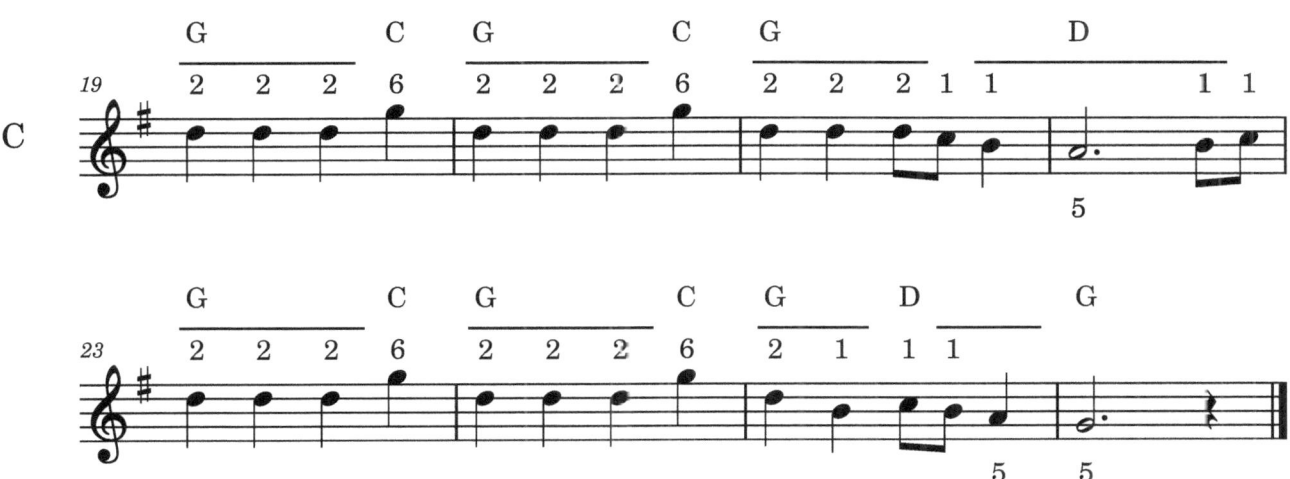

Grandfather's Tune

Buttons played

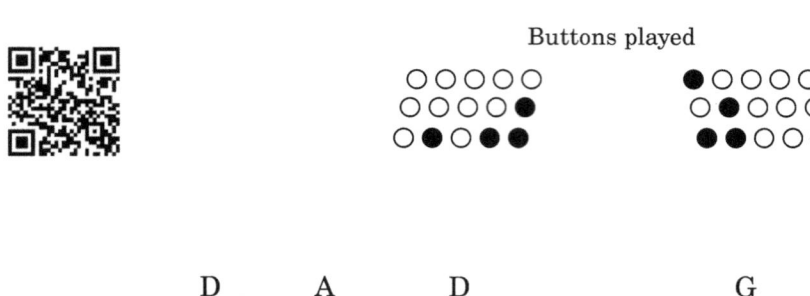

Traditional

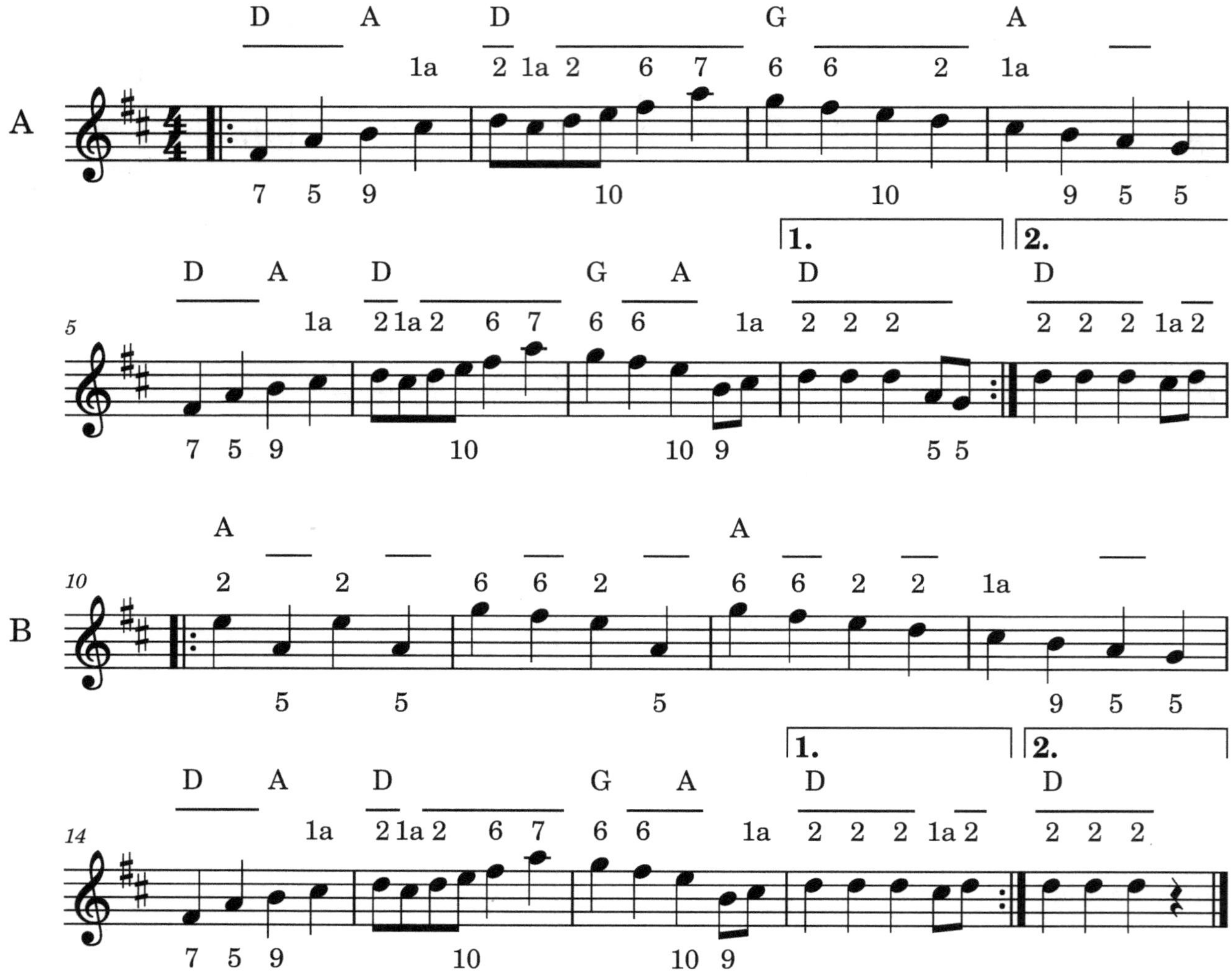

Harper's Frolic

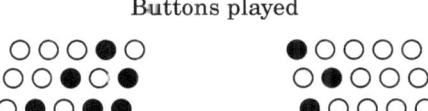

Traditional

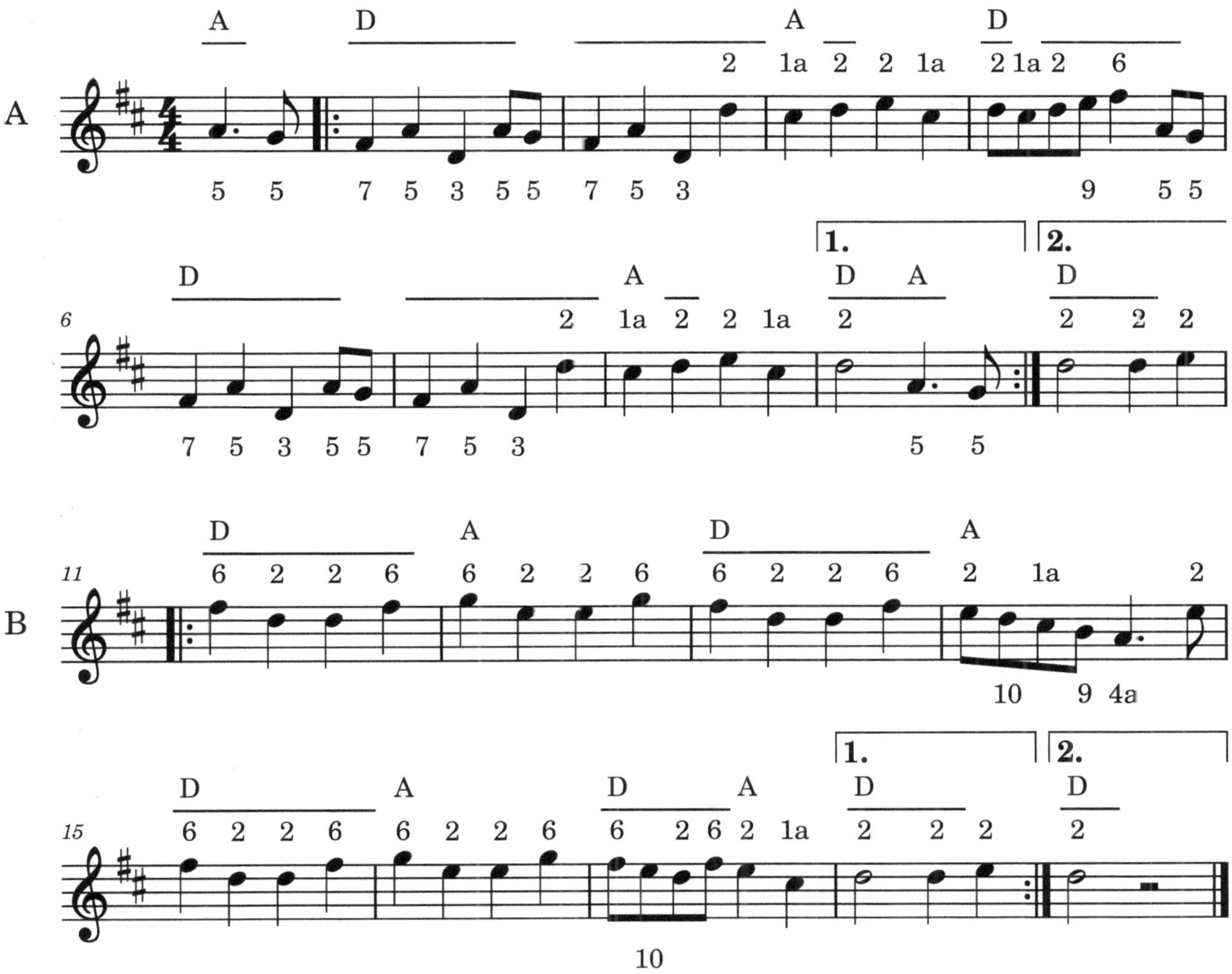

Horses Brawl (Branle des Chevaux)

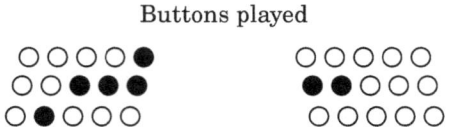

Traditional

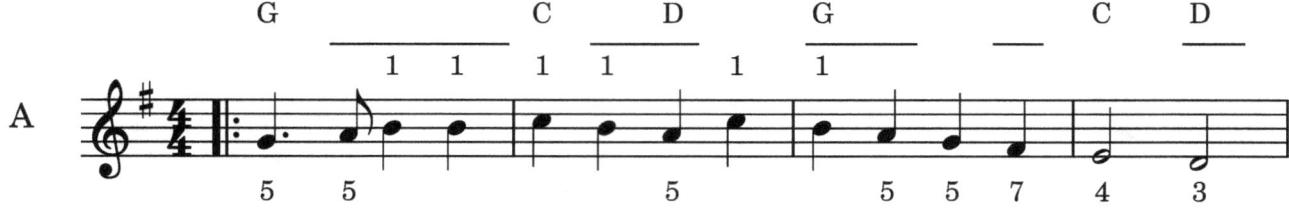

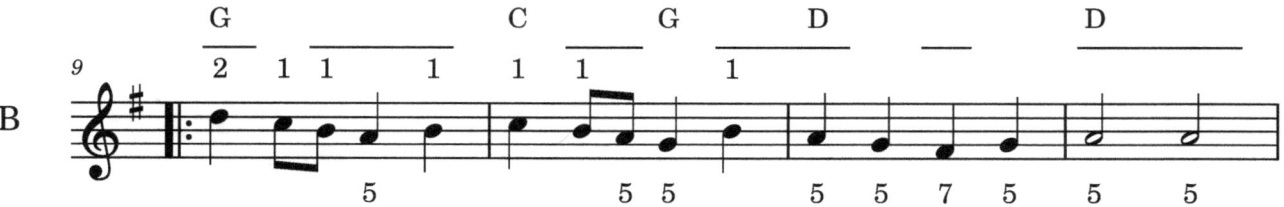
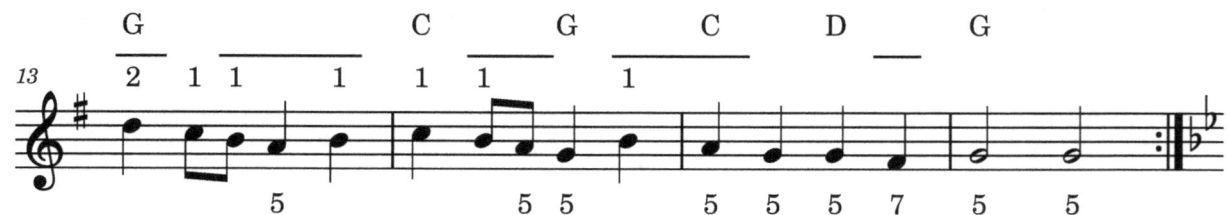

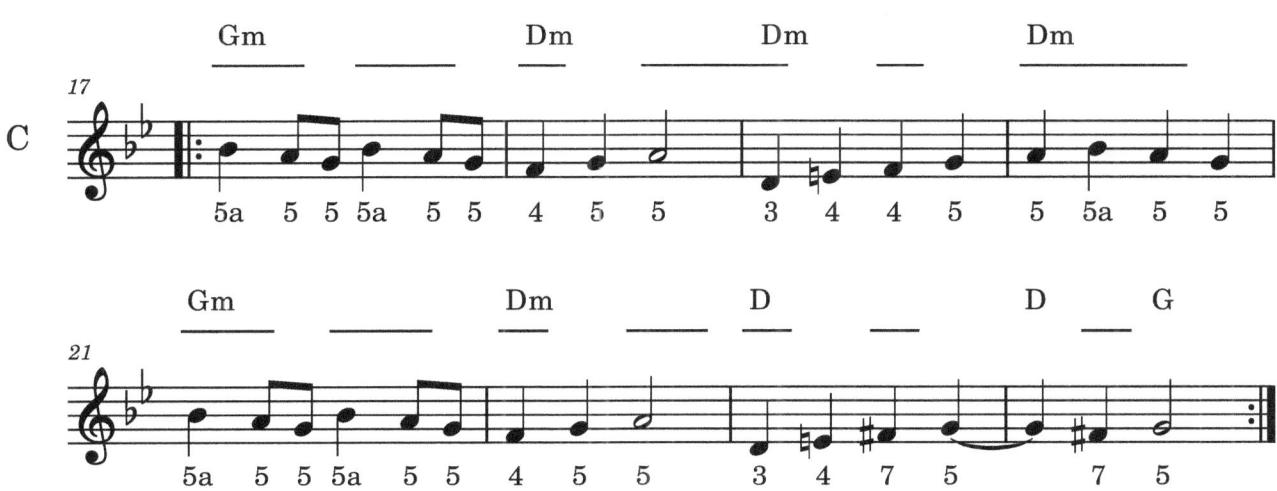

Hunting the Hare

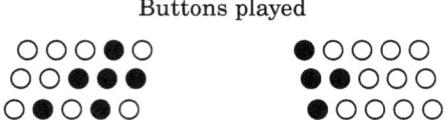

Buttons played

Traditional

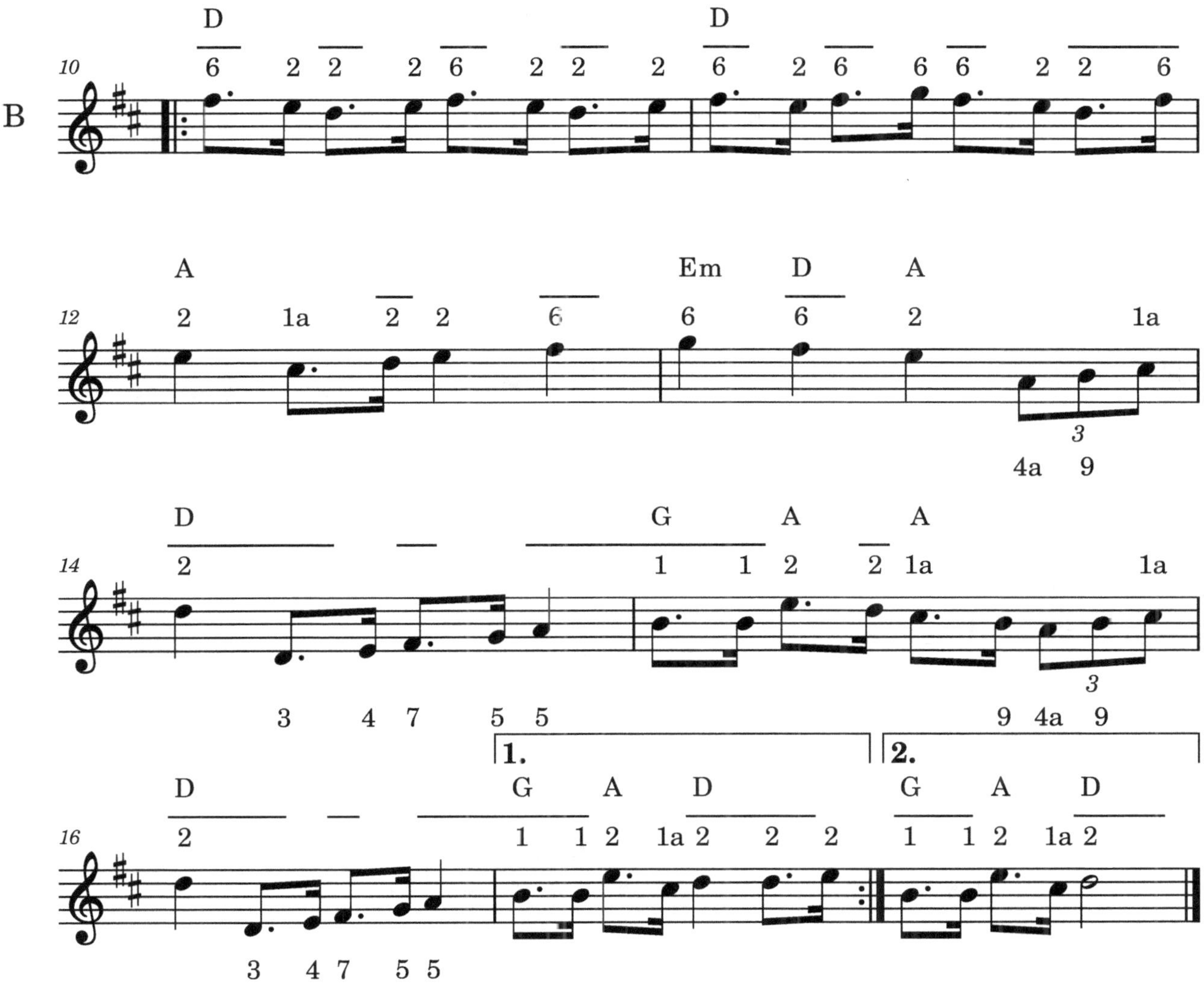

Huntsman's Chorus

Buttons played

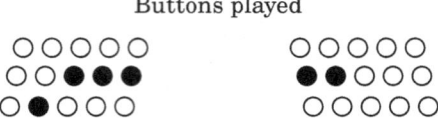

Carl Maria von Weber (1821)

Jamie Allen

Buttons played

Traditional

Jenny Lind

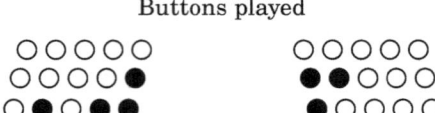

Traditional

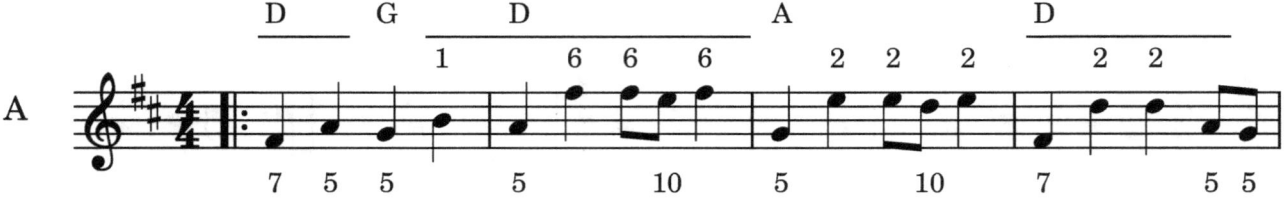

Keel Row

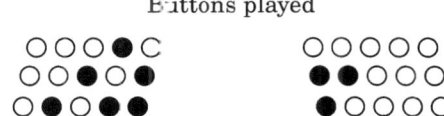

Traditional

Traditional English Session Tunes

Lemmy Brazil's No.2

Buttons played

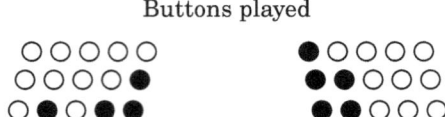

Traditional

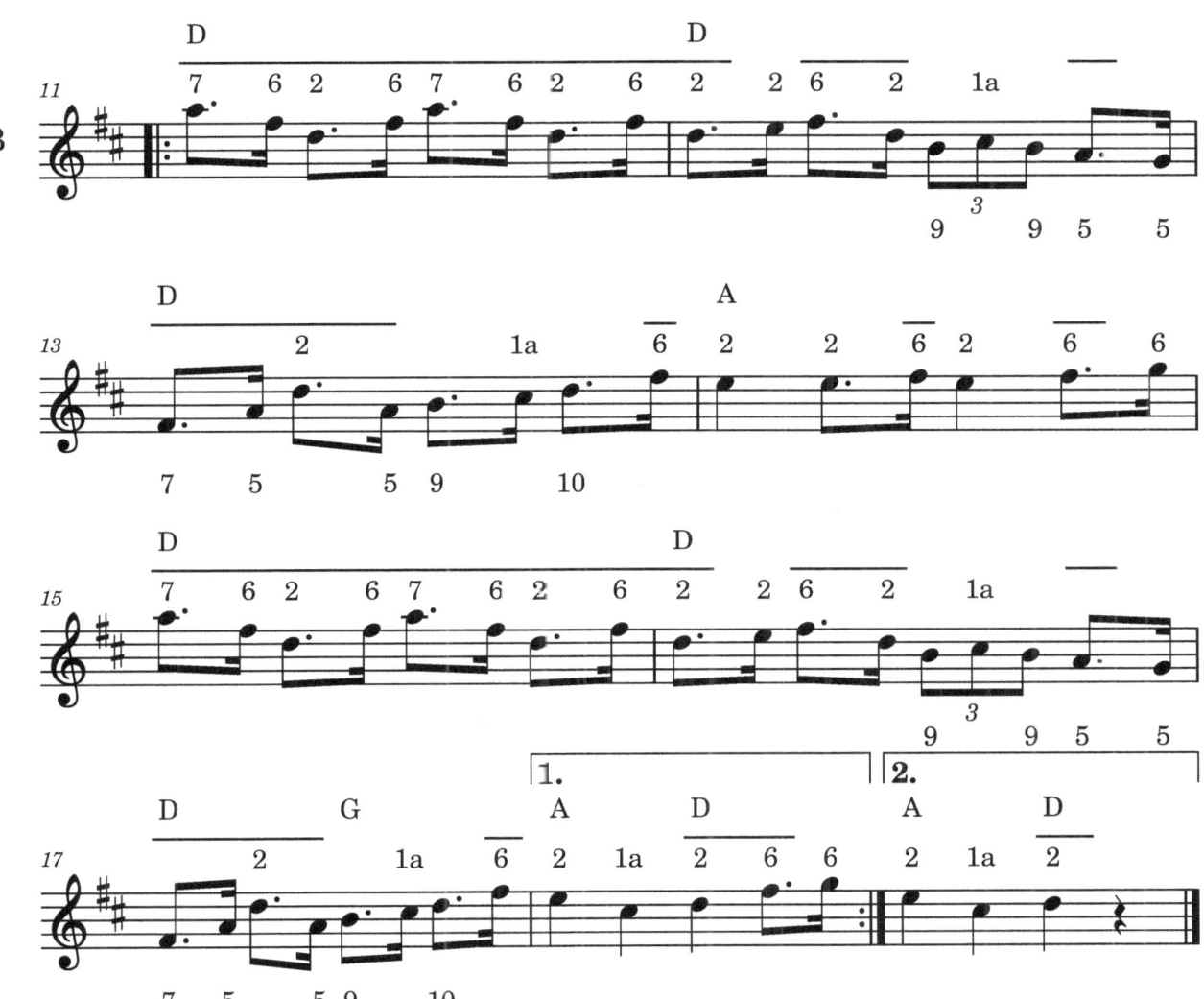

Linnen Hall

Buttons played

Traditional

Little Diamond

 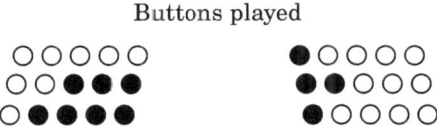 

Traditional

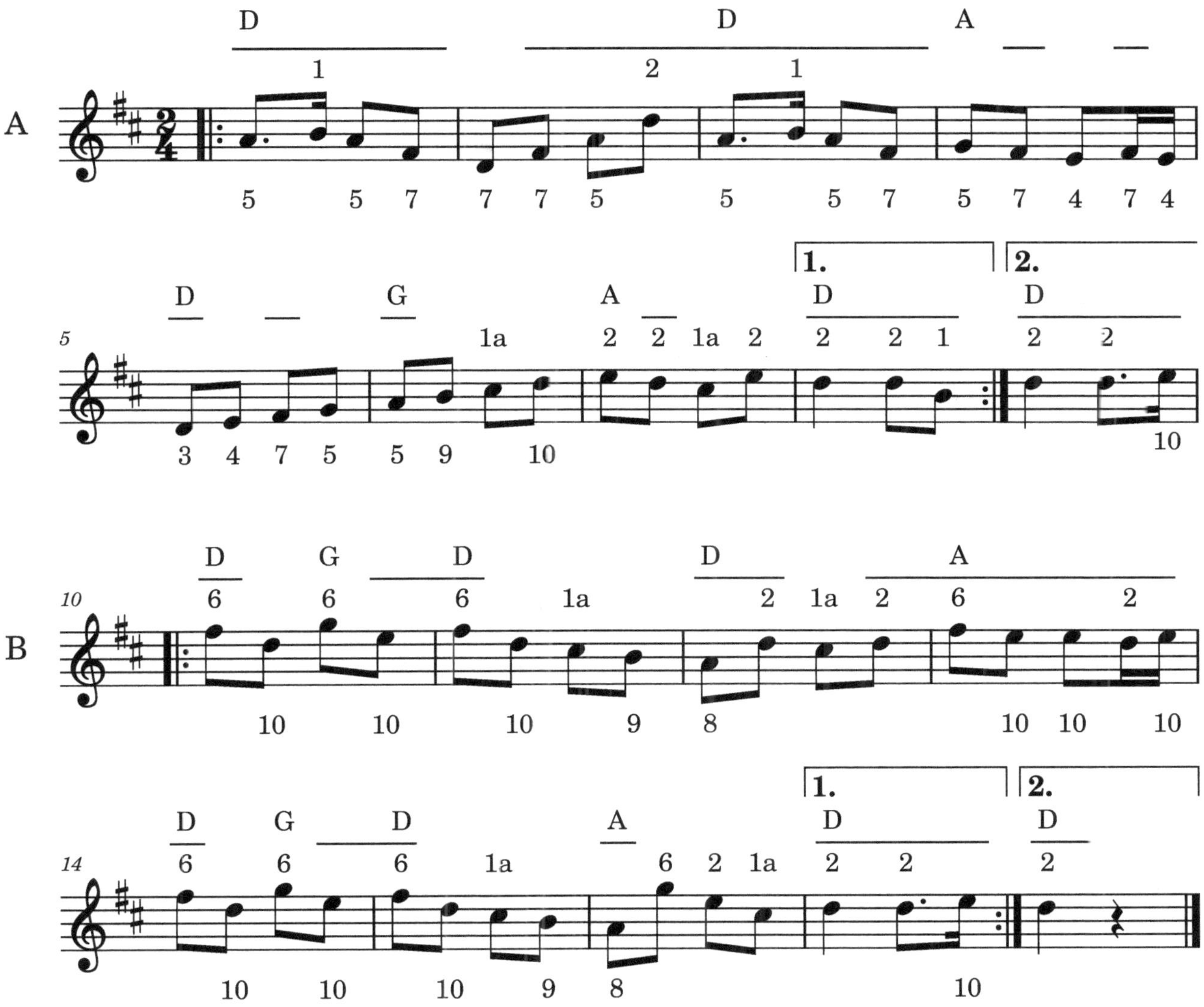

The Man in the Moon

Michael Turner's Waltz

Buttons played
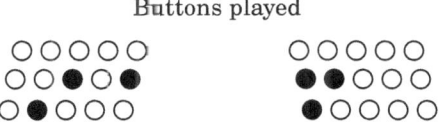

Mozart (KV536 No.2)

New Rigged Ship

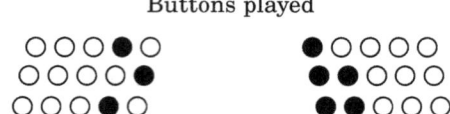

Buttons played

Traditional

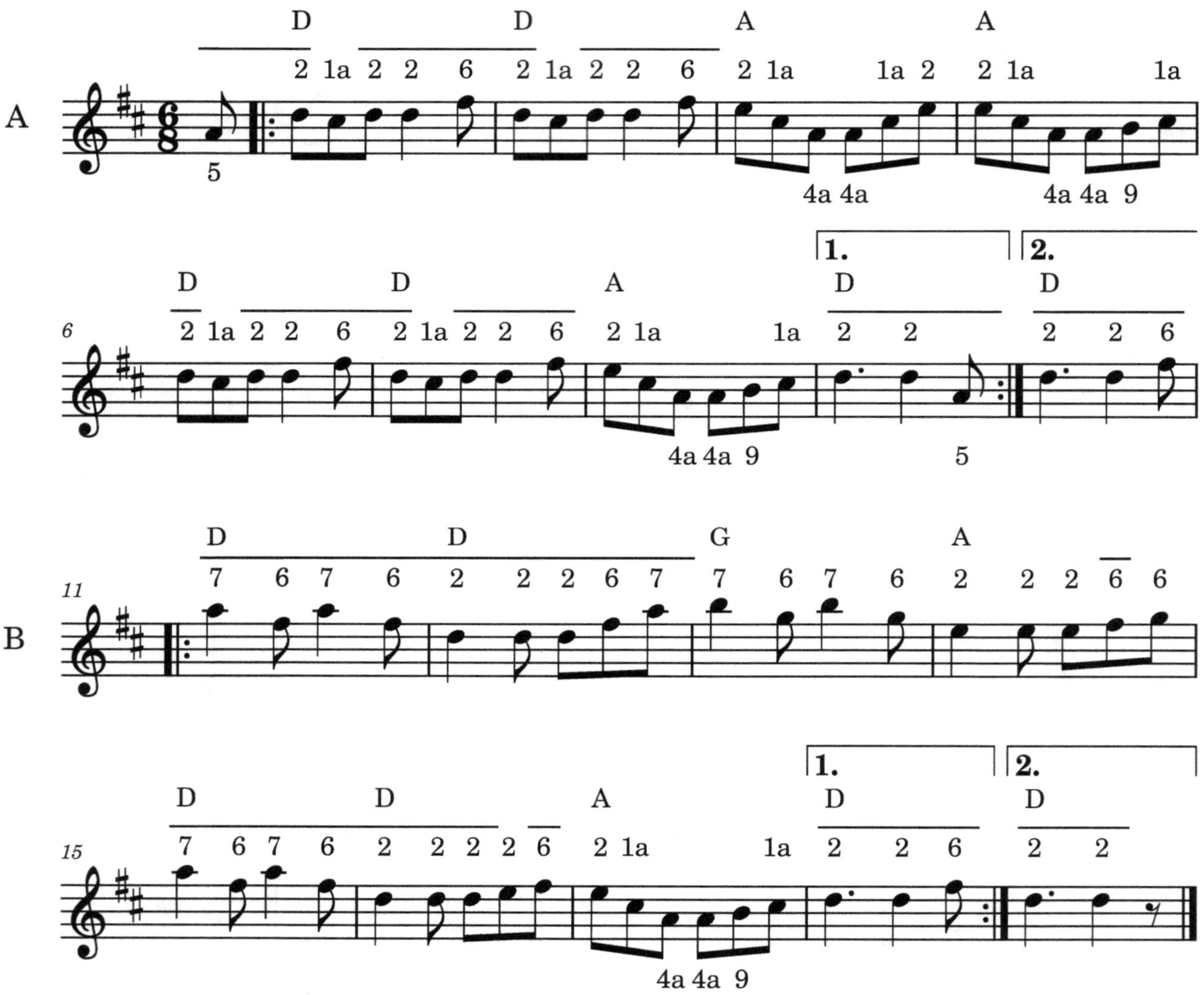

Off She Goes

Buttons played

Traditional

Orange in Bloom

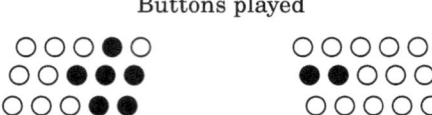

Buttons played

Traditional

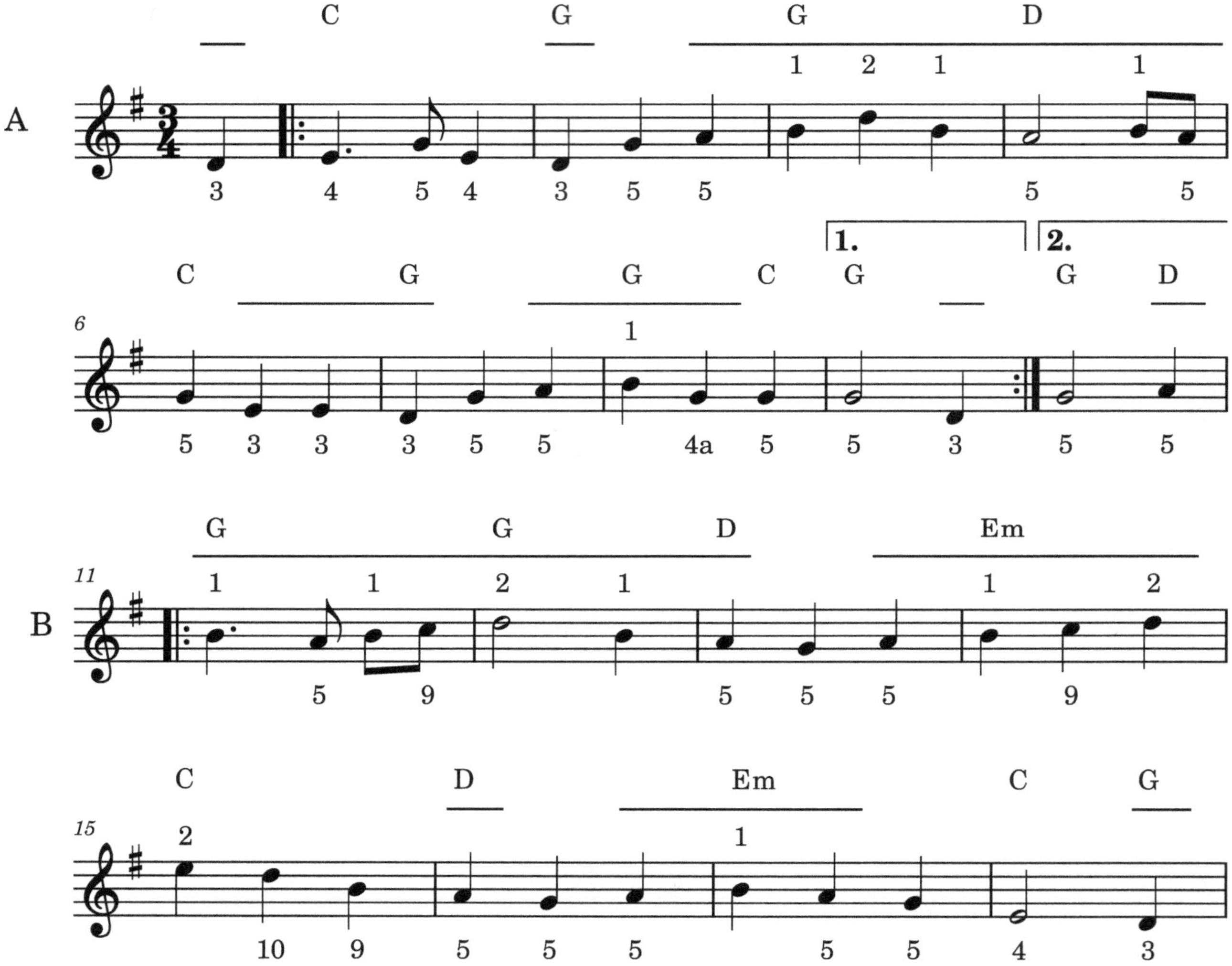

Traditional English Session Tunes

The Oyster Girl

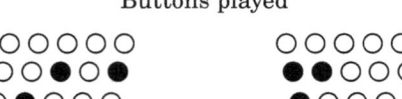

Traditional

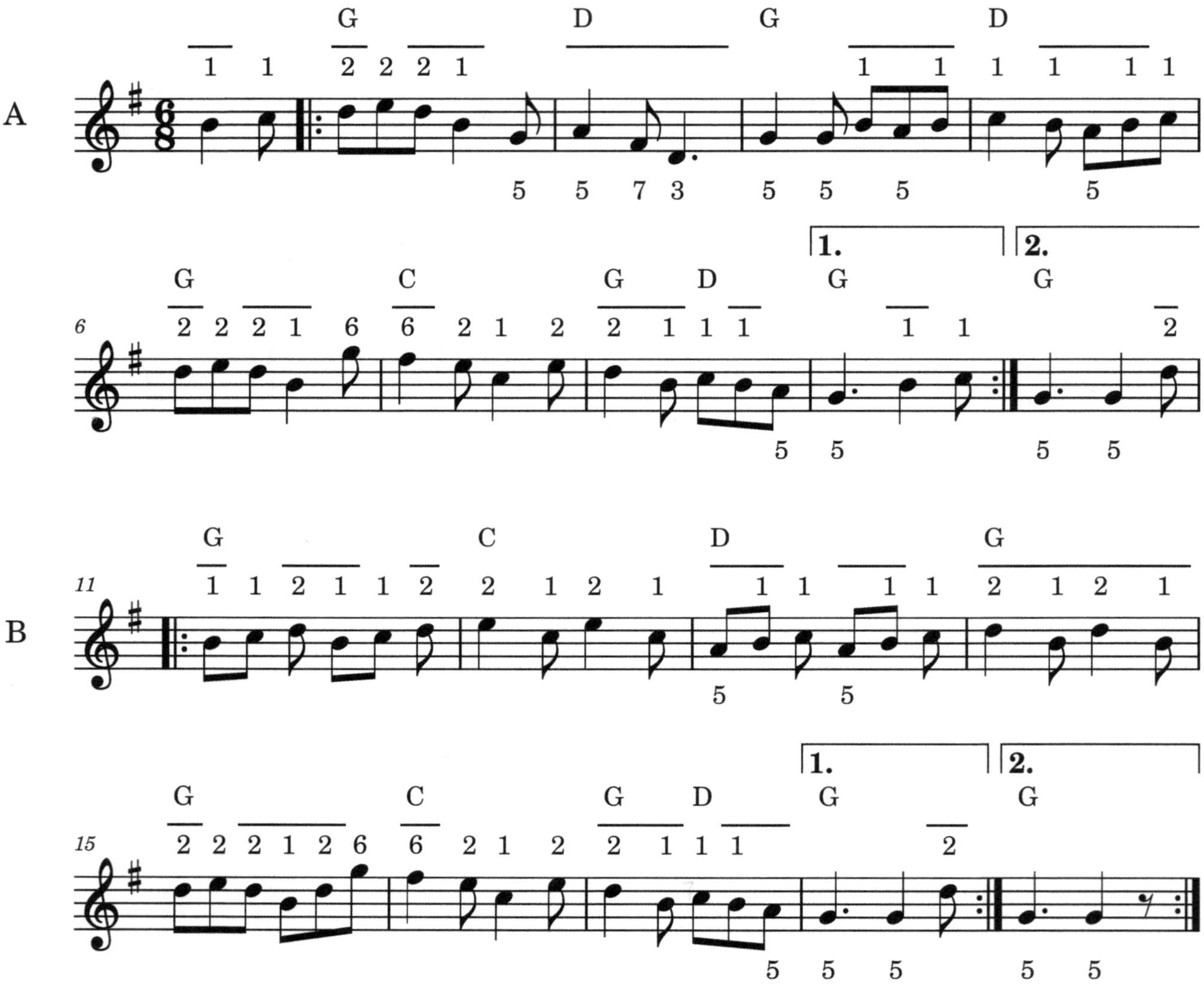

Portsmouth

Buttons played

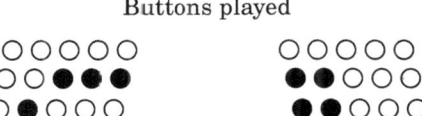

Traditional

Princess Royal

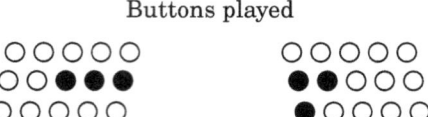

Buttons played

Traditional

The Quaker

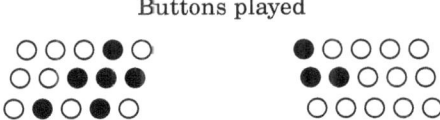

Traditional

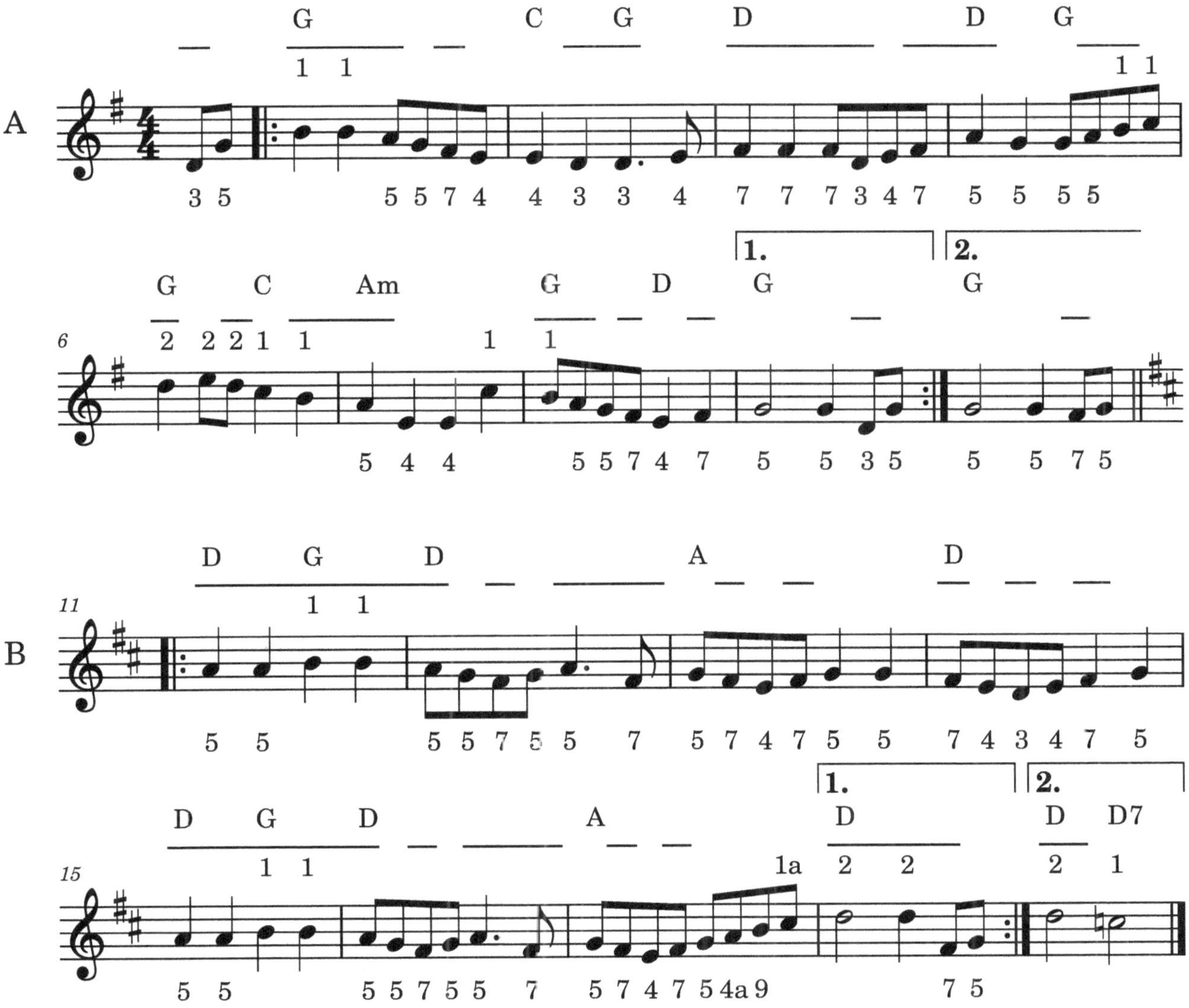

The Railway

Buttons played

Traditional

Rakes of Mallow

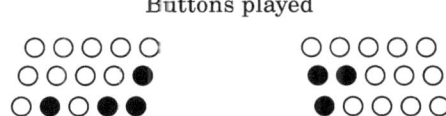

Buttons played

Traditional

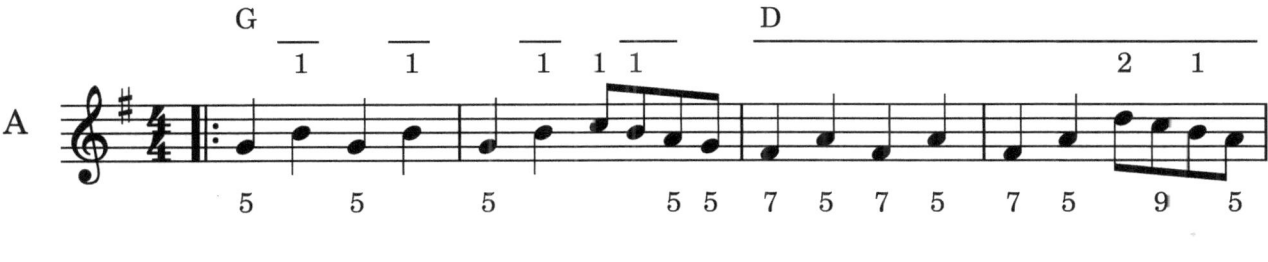
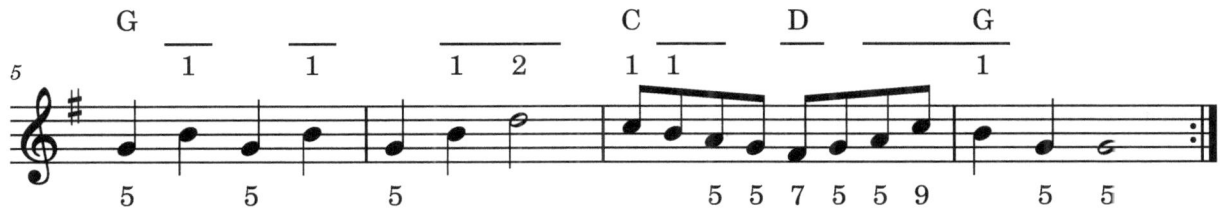

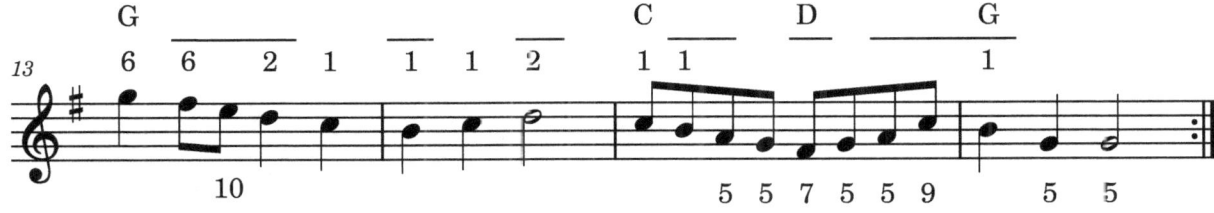

Traditional English Session Tunes

The Redowa Polka

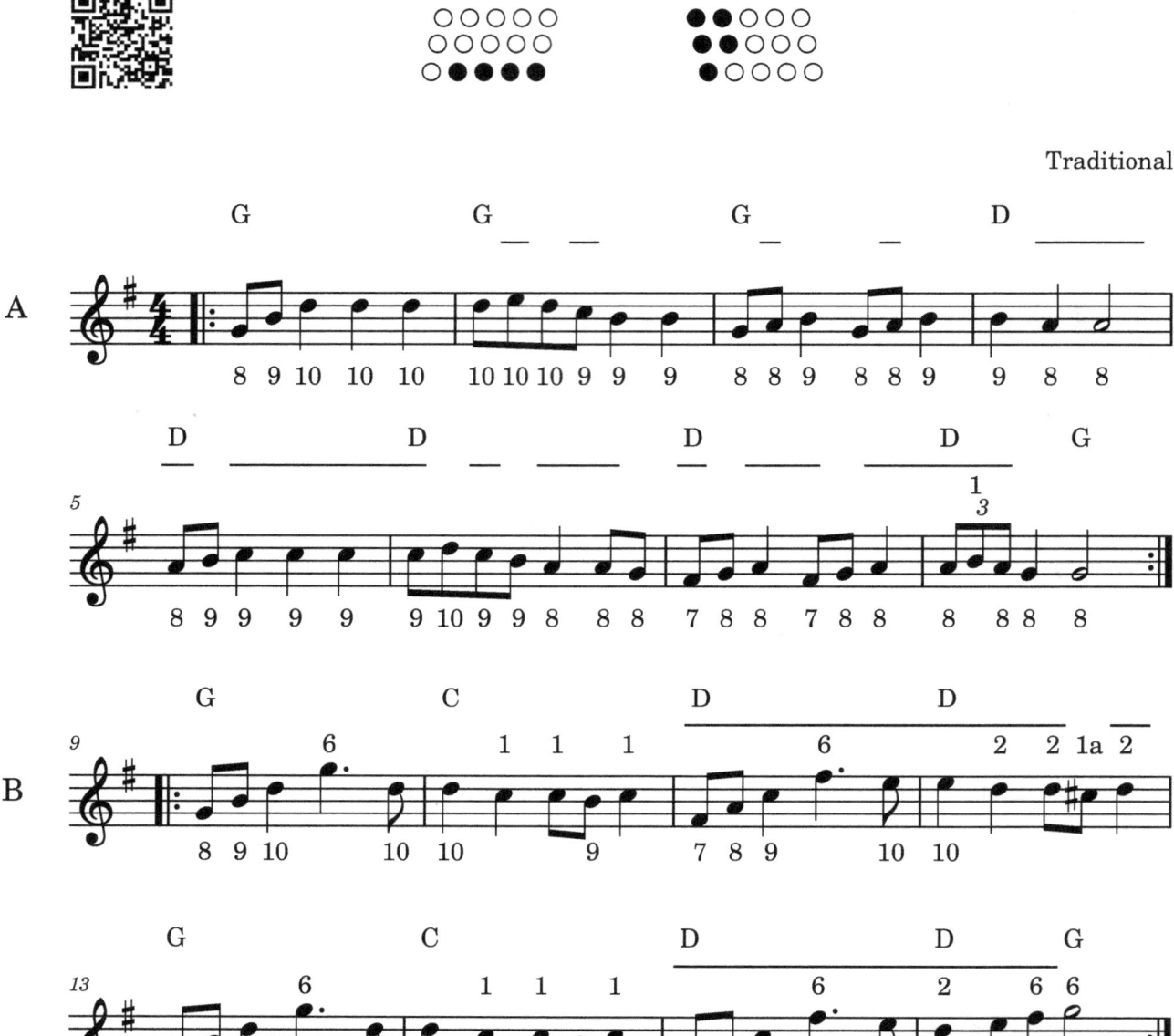

Traditional English Session Tunes

Rochdale Coconut Dance

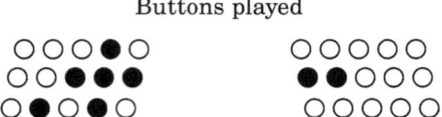

Traditional

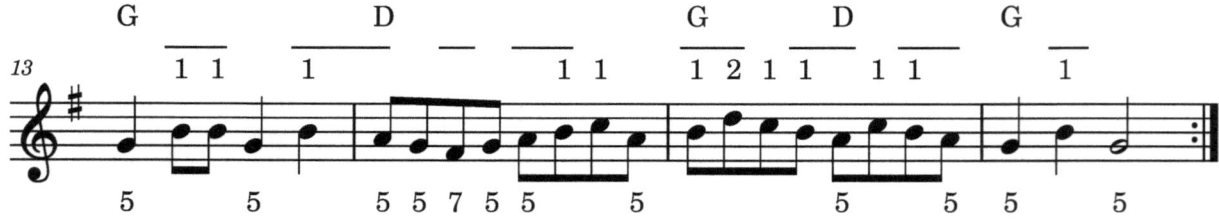

Traditional English Session Tunes

Rogues March

Buttons played

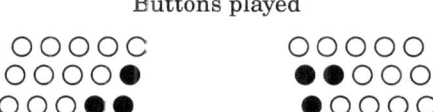

Traditional

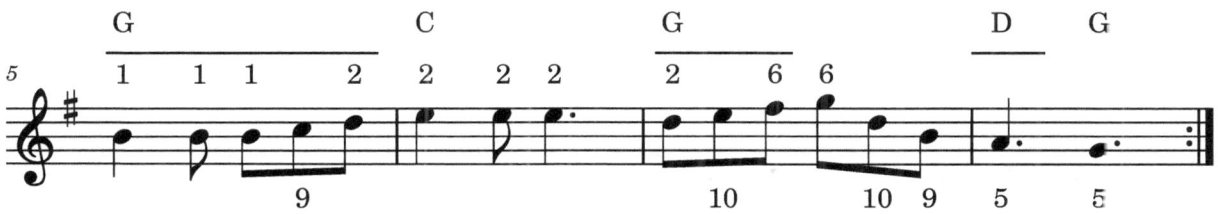
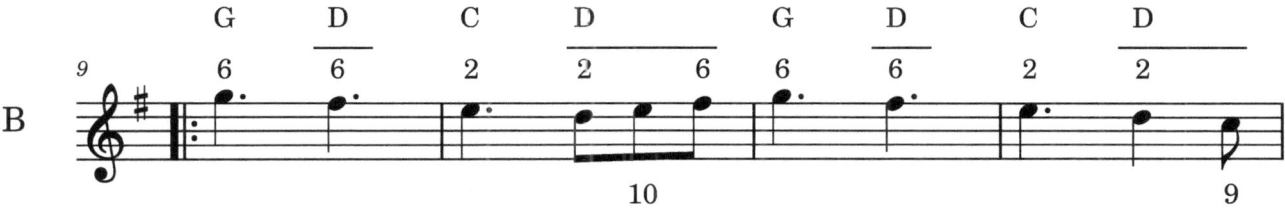

Traditional English Session Tunes

Roman Wall

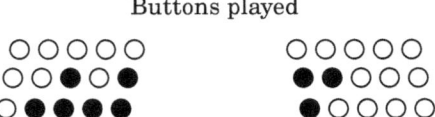

Traditional

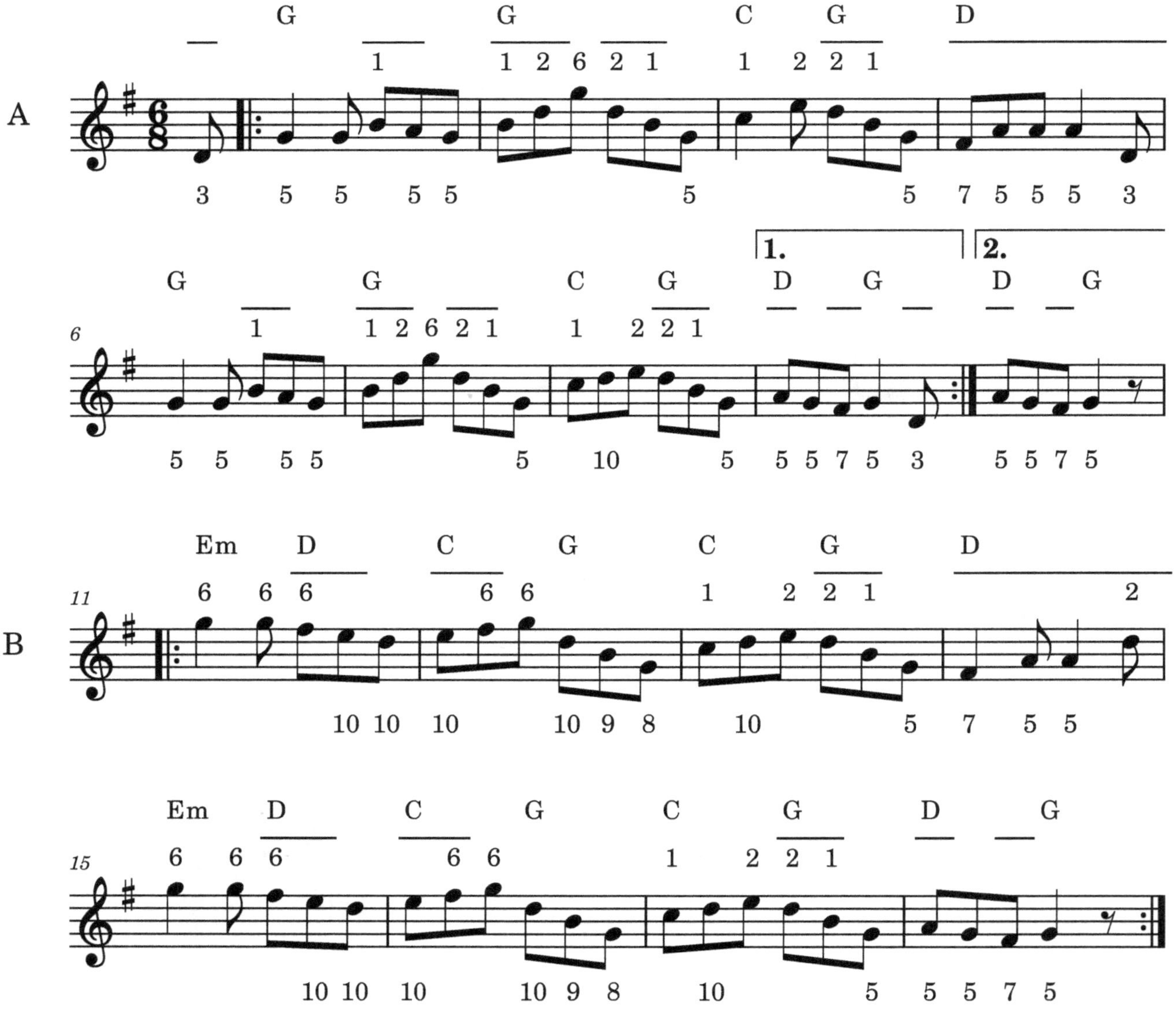

The Rose Tree

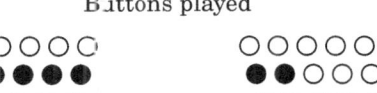

Traditional

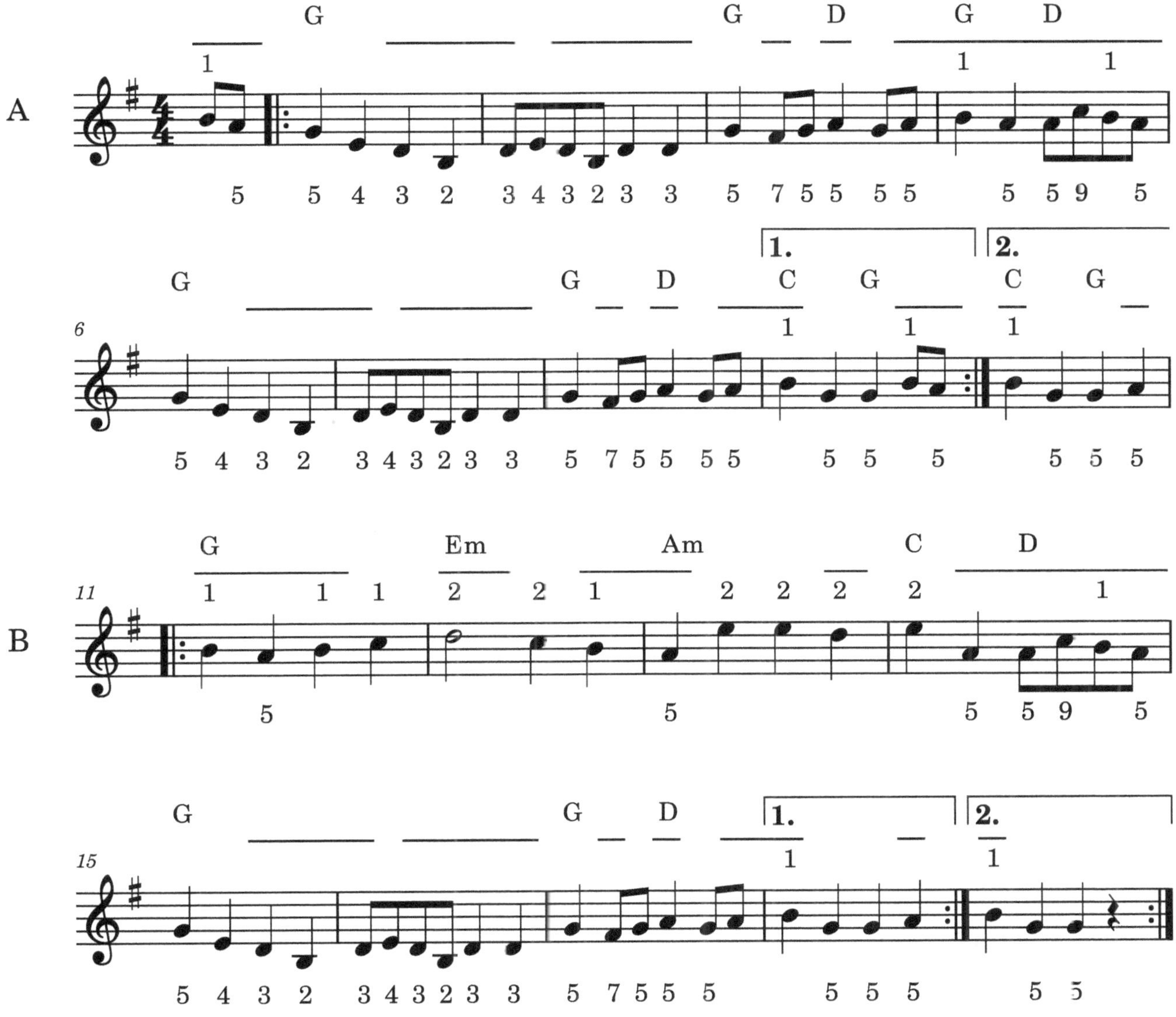

Roxburgh Castle

Buttons played

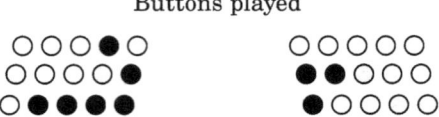

Traditional

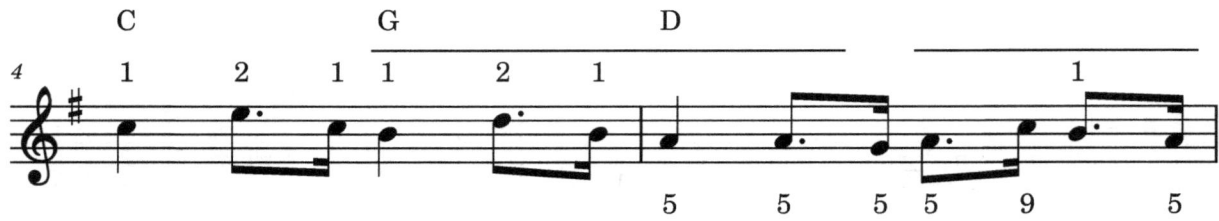

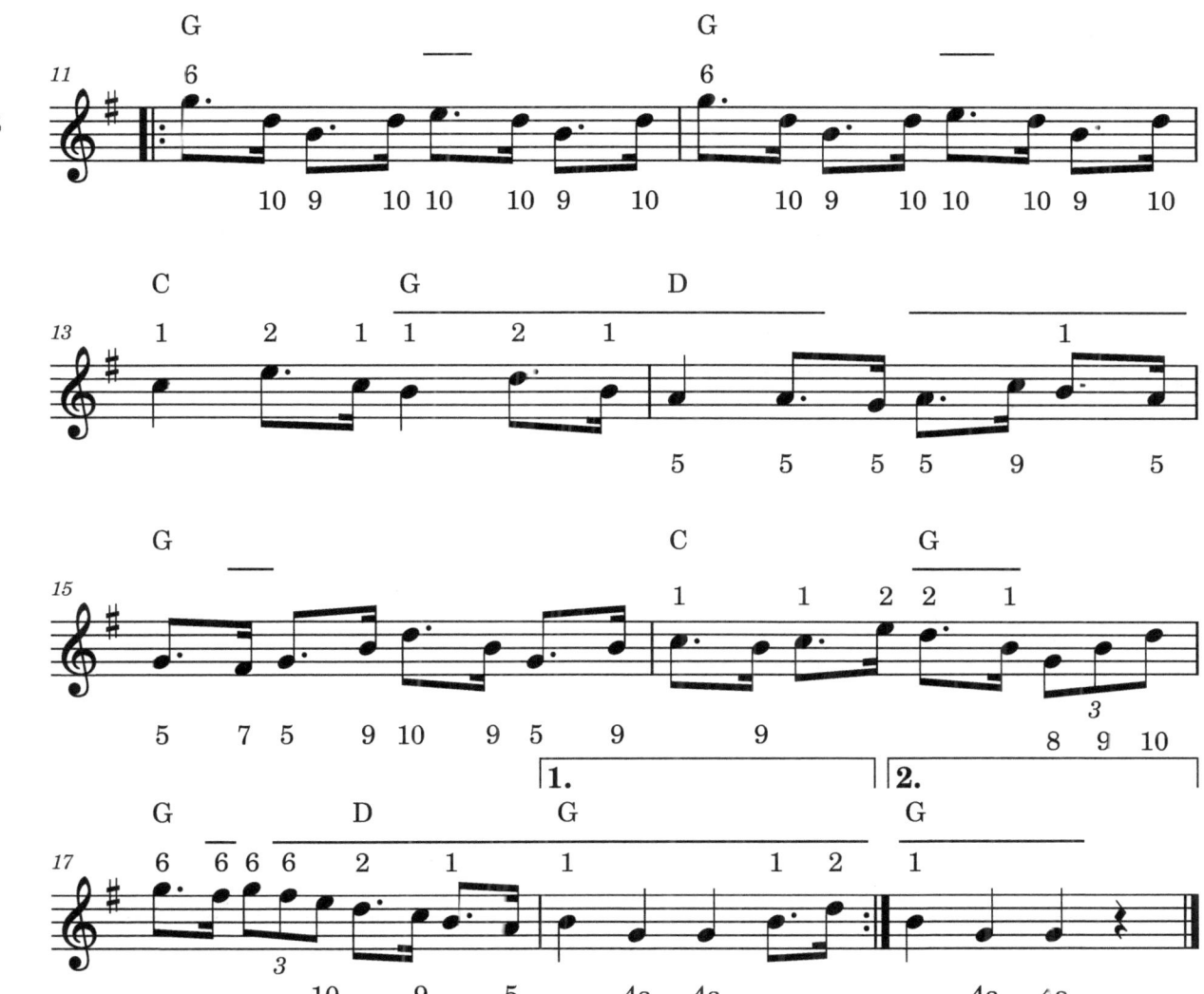

Salmon Tails Up the Water

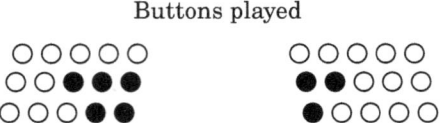

Buttons played

Traditional

Scan Tester's Polka No.2

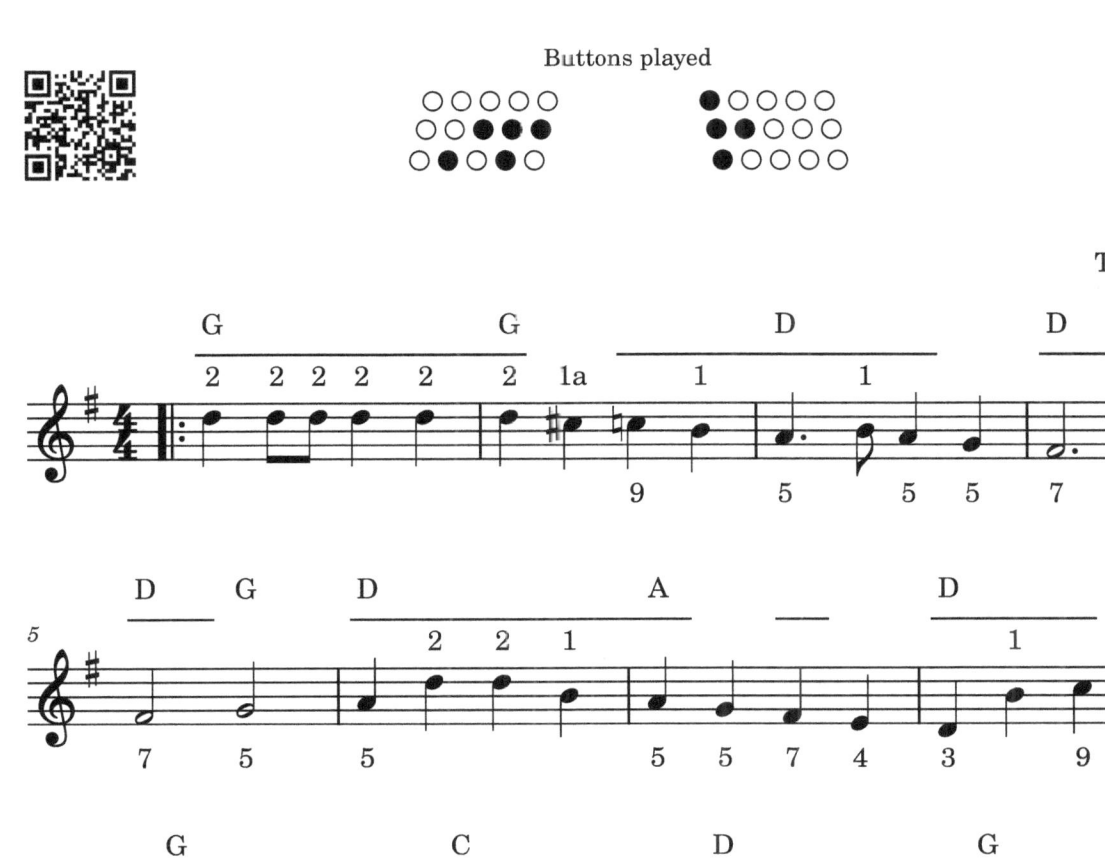

Traditional English Session Tunes 75

The Seven Stars

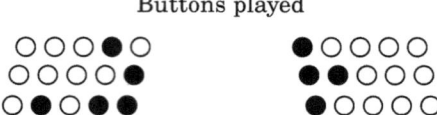

The Shepton Mallet Hornpipe

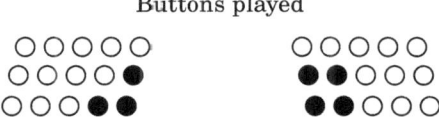

Buttons played

Traditional

Traditional English Session Tunes

The Sloe

Buttons played

 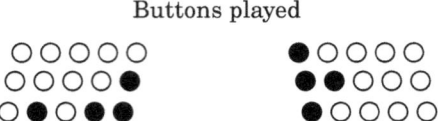 

Traditional

Smash the Windows

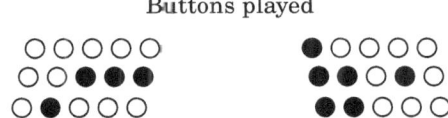

Traditional

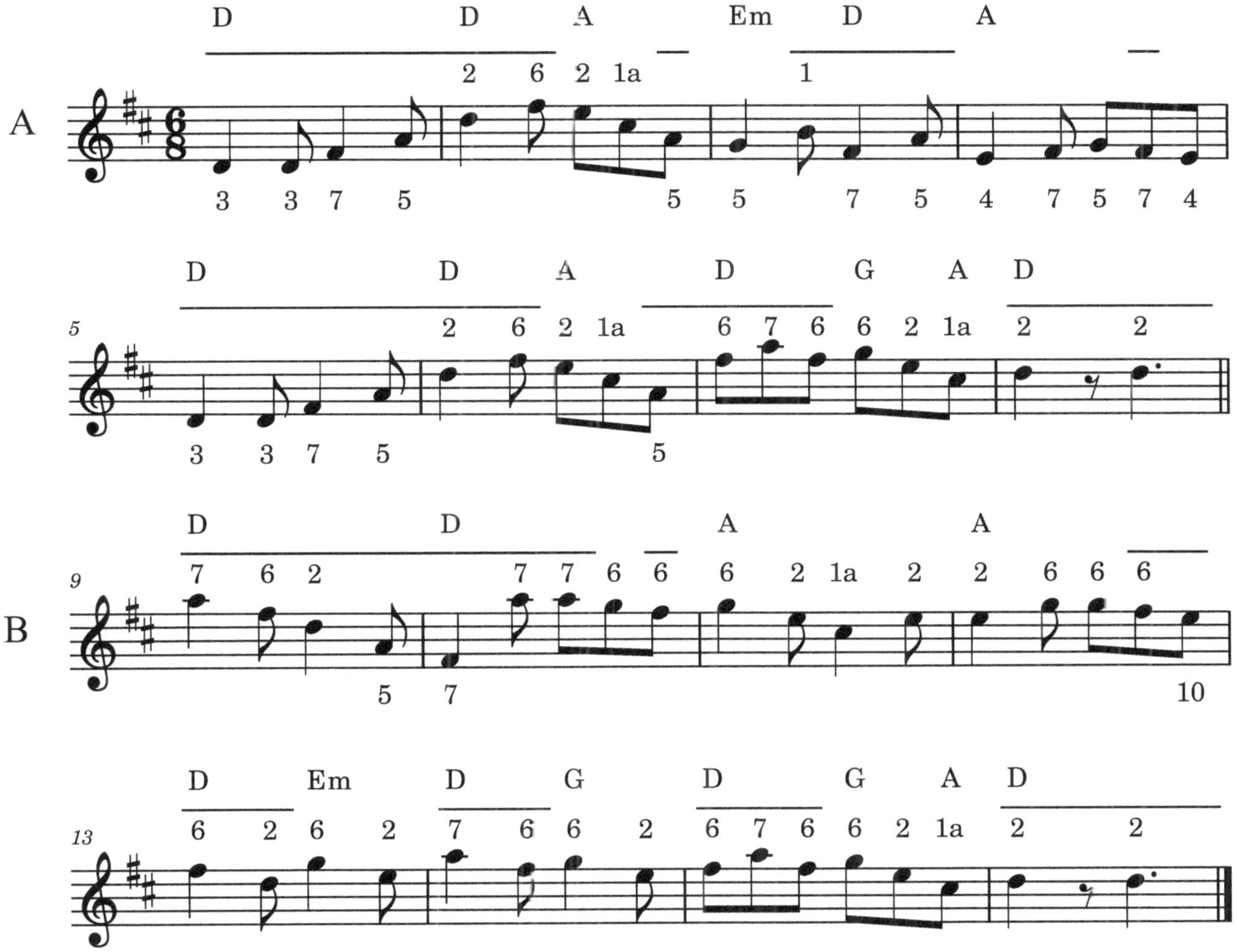

Speed the Plough

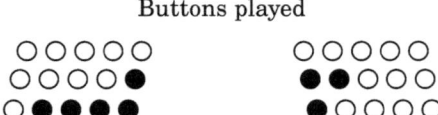

Traditional

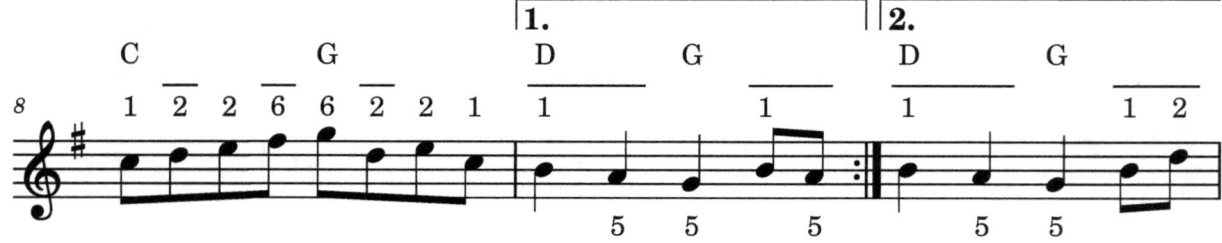

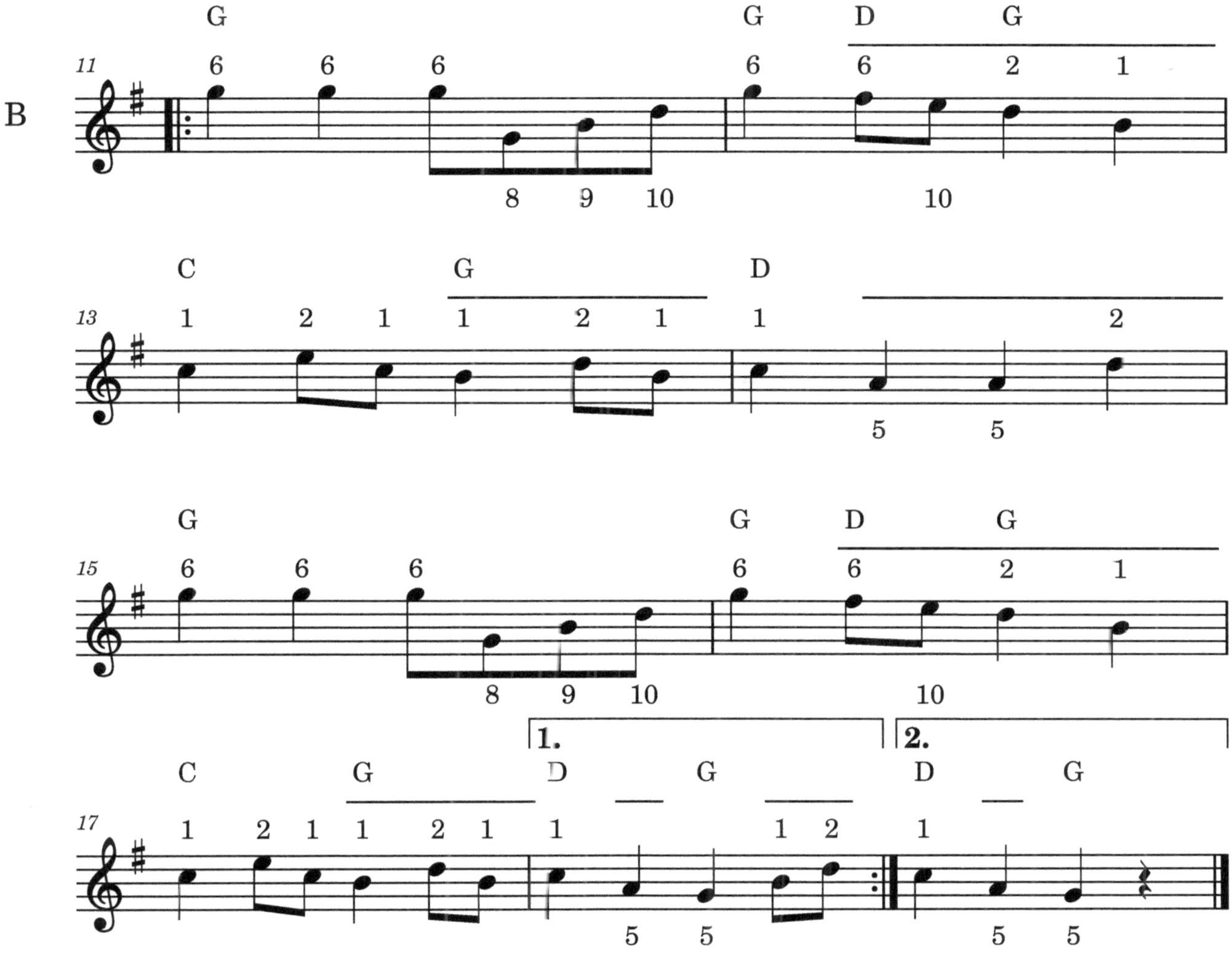
B
G G D G
C G D
G G D G
C G 1. D G 2. D G

Three Around Three

Buttons played

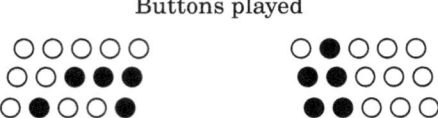

Traditional

Tip Top Polka

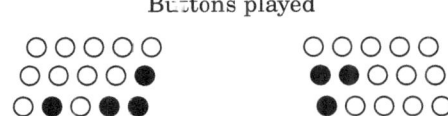

Traditional English Session Tunes

Uncle Bernard's

Buttons played

Traditional

Walter Bulwer's No.1

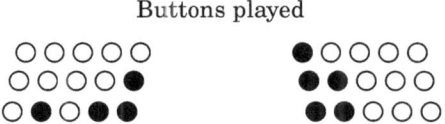

Traditional

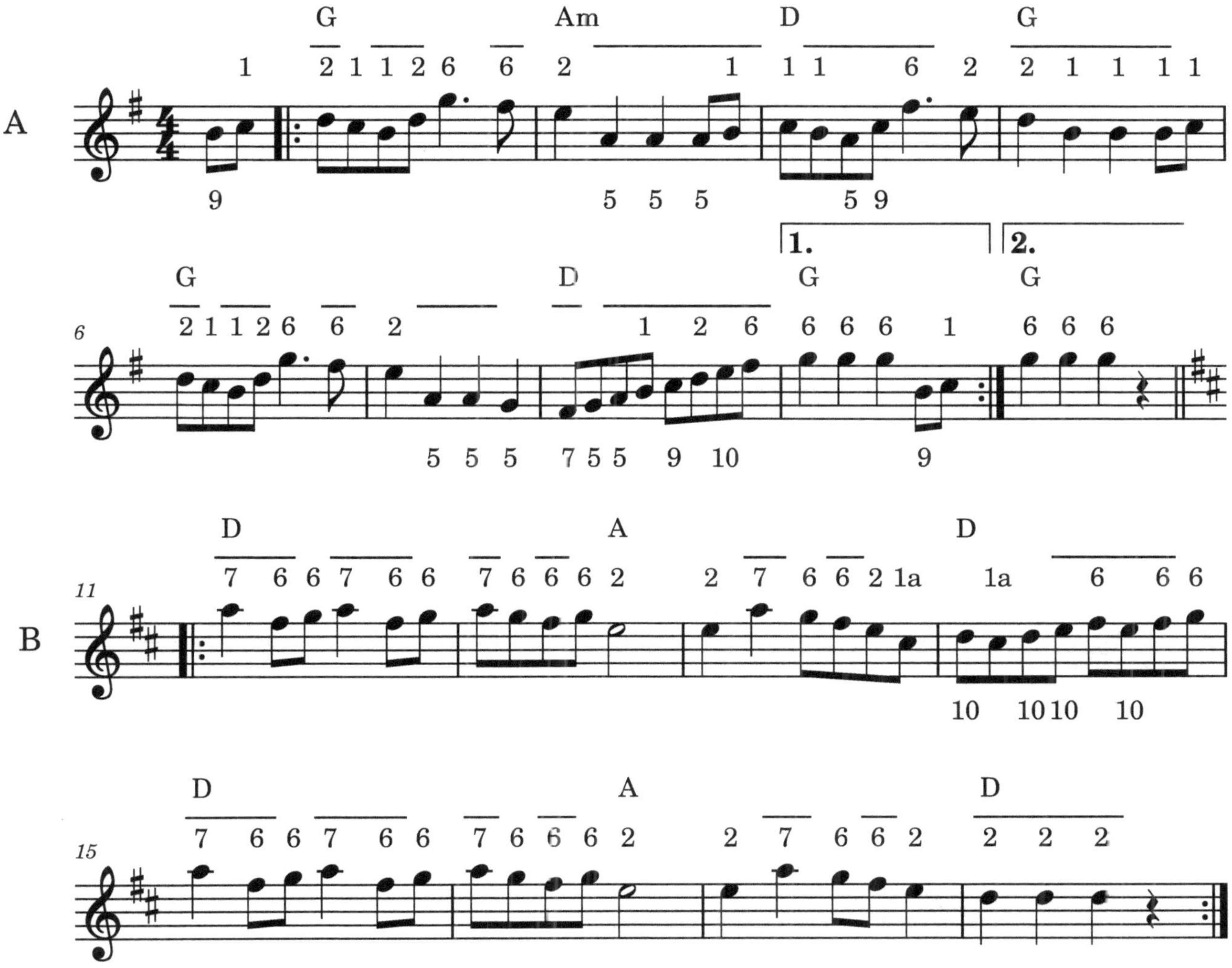

Walter Bulwer's No.2

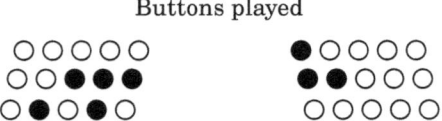

Buttons played

Traditional

Winster Gallop

Buttons played

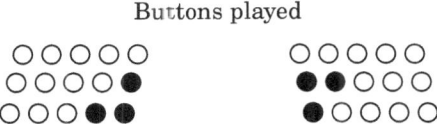

Traditional

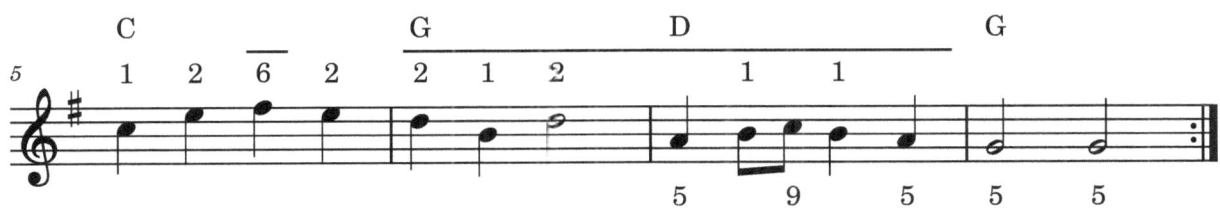
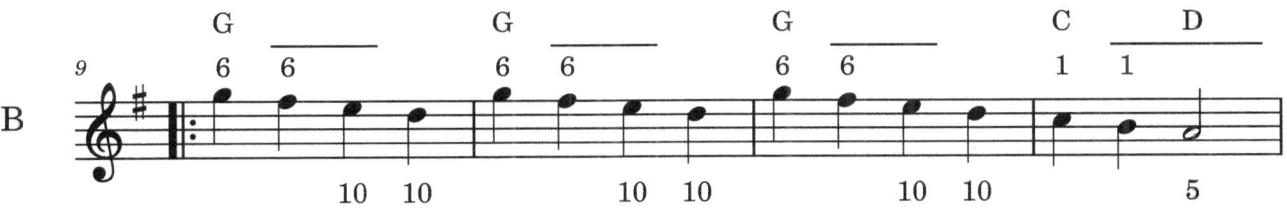
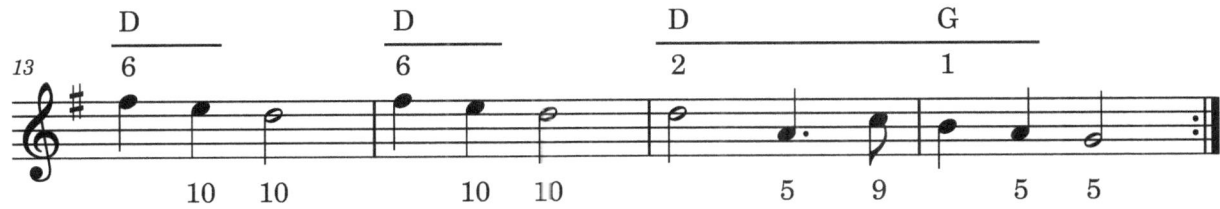

Traditional English Session Tunes

Woodland Revels

Traditional English Session Tunes

The Young May Moon

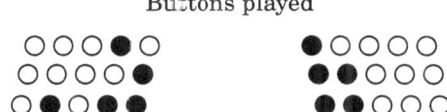

Buttons played

Traditional

Gary Coover

A longtime fan of the concertina ever since discovering British traditional music while in college, Gary was inspired to learn to play the Anglo concertina through the music of John Kirkpatrick and John Watcham. In addition to Anglo, he also plays English and Jeffries Duet concertinas, as well as D/G melodeon.

He hosted and produced the popular "Shepherd's Hey" radio program of British Isles traditional music on KPFT FM-90.1 in Houston, Texas, for over 15 years.

Gary was a founding member of The Four Bricks out of Hadrian's Wall where he played concertina, melodeon, keyboards and bass, and he was also an original member of The Men of Houston Morris Dance team.

In 2013 he published his first Anglo instruction book, *Anglo Concertina in the Harmonic Style*, which included tunes from William Kimber, John Kirkpatrick, Jody Kruskal, Bertram Levy, Kenneth Loveless, Brian Peters, Andy Turner, and John Watcham.

The success of this book led to the creation of Rollston Press, which today has nearly 50 titles in its catalog, many of which are instruction books for a wide variety of music especially arranged for the Anglo concertina.

All of Gary's books utilize a simple and popular "play-by-number" tablature system based on 19th century Anglo tutors. Most of the books feature video instruction – Rollston Press was the first music publisher to incorporate QR code links that provide video and audio links to YouTube videos and SoundCloud audio recordings.

Concertina Books from Rollston Press

Anglo Concertina in the Harmonic Style

Easy Anglo 1-2-3

Christmas Concertina

Civil War Concertina

75 Irish Session Tunes for Anglo Concertina

A Garden of Dainty Delights

Pirate Songs for Concertina

Sailor Songs for Concertina

Sea Songs for 20-Button Anglo Concertina

Cowboy Concertina

A Garden of Dainty Delights

The Jeffries Duet Concertina Tutor

The Anglo Concertina Music of John Watcham

The Anglo Concertina Music of John Kirkpatrick

The Anglo Concertina Music of Phil Ham

Anglo Concertina from Beginner to Master

House Dance

Chris Droney of Bell Harbour

Handbook of Tunes and Methods for Irish Traditional Music

The Anglo Concertina Music of Alan Day

75 *More* Irish Session Tunes for Anglo Concertina

19th Century Anglo

Praise the Lord and Pass the Concertina

The Anglo Concertina Music of William Kimber

AVAILABLE FROM AMAZON,
RED COW MUSIC (UK), AND OTHER FINE RETAILERS

www.ingramcontent.com/pod-product-compliance
Lightning Source LLC
Chambersburg PA
CBHW081136170426
43197CB00017B/2878